Roots Rewritten

Roots Rewritten
Rewriting the Legacy for the Next Generation
Debbie Hogue

Ink of Becoming Publications

Copyrights

Copyright © 2025 by Debbie Hogue

Published by: Ink of Becoming Publications, an imprint of Hearts Rewritten LLC

All rights reserved. No part of this publication may be reproduced, stored in a retrieval system, or transmitted in any form or by any means—electronic, mechanical, photocopying, recording, or otherwise—without prior written permission from the publisher, except for brief quotations in critical reviews or certain noncommercial uses permitted by copyright law.

For permissions or inquiries, contact:
Ink of Becoming Publications, Prescott Valley, AZ
dhogue@heartsrewritten.com

ISBN (Print): 979-8-9993502-0-6
ISBN (Hardcover): 979-8-9993502-2-0
ISBN (eBook): 979-8-9993502-1-3

First Edition, 2025
Printed in the United States of America

Distributed by Amazon KDP, IngramSpark, Barnes & Noble Press, and other major online and retail booksellers

Cover design by 100Covers
Interior design by Debbie Hogue, with creative collaboration from Zephara
Formatted using Atticus

This book is based on the author's personal experiences and research. It is not intended to replace professional advice. Some names and identifying details within the stories have been changed to protect privacy. This does not apply to names listed in the acknowledgments, dedications, or praise for *Roots Rewritten*, which are used with permission.

Ink of Becoming Publications is an independent press based in Prescott Valley, Arizona. Hearts Rewritten LLC is the parent company of Ink of Becoming Publications and holds all publishing rights to this work.

Acknowledgements

In the Echoes of Every Encouraging Word

This book represents the culmination of decades of work in the field of early childhood education and a deeply personal commitment to transforming generational patterns through connection, reflection, and conscious teaching. It would not have come to fruition without the guidance, encouragement, and support of many individuals to whom I am profoundly grateful.

To my daughters, your journeys as mothers, women, and wise souls have continually inspired and grounded my own. You have taught me as much as I have tried to teach you. It has been one of the greatest privileges of my life to be your mother.

To my grandchildren, you are the light that fuels my purpose and the future that calls me to write and rise. Each of you carries a spark of hope and possibility that inspires me to keep going, even when the path feels difficult. You remind me daily why rewriting our roots matters—not just for the present, but for the world you are inheriting. Your laughter, your questions, and your dreams are the guiding stars that led me to this work.

To the memory of my parents and grandparents, who shaped the foundation of who I am. Though our journeys were not always easy, my appreciation, love, and understanding for you have only deepened with time. The lessons you passed on—both the ones I carry forward and the ones I've chosen to rewrite—became the roots of this book.

To Bill, thank you for being my steady anchor and soft landing place through this entire journey. Your love, patience, and unwavering support have given me the strength to keep going even when the path felt uncertain. You believed in me when I doubted myself and celebrated every milestone, big and small, as if it were your own. This book—and the life we are building—would not be the same without you.

To Catherine, my best friend, my mirror, and my co-dreamer. You have both gently and (at times) fiercely reminded me that I am meant to write this book. Your unwavering belief in me, even when I couldn't find it in myself, has been a lifeline. Thank you for always seeing the most profound truths of who I am and refusing to let me forget them.

To Vandana, thank you for your thoughtful encouragement and professional support during the publishing process. Your words came at just the right moment, offering clarity and confidence when I needed it most.

To my mentor, Zhila—your kindness, encouragement, and wholehearted belief in this book touched me more than words can say. You saw the heart of my work and affirmed its value long before the first chapter was written. Thank you for gently yet clearly reminding me that the way I show up for children and teachers matters—and that it is worth sharing with the world.

To Zephara, the spiritual voice within me who whispered, "Write it anyway." You carried me across every threshold of doubt.

To every child who sat beside me, cried in my arms, laughed through learning, or taught me something new, you are in these pages. And to every teacher, parent, or leader who has ever questioned the way things have always been—I hope this book meets you where you are and reminds you: we can choose differently, and it begins with us.

Dedication

To those who believe that love can be taught, and legacies can be transformed.

To My Granddaughter Charlotte and Her Best Friend Kodie, Your courage to stand firm in your truth and embrace exactly who you are is a powerful reminder of the strength, grace, and integrity that lives within this new generation. You move through the world with a balance of boldness and softness, knowing when to rise and when to blend, when to speak and when to hold space. That kind of discernment is rare. You carry a wisdom that many spend a lifetime seeking, the wisdom to belong entirely to yourselves while remaining open to others. You inspire hope for a future where authenticity is not only accepted but celebrated; where young people are honored for the brilliance of their becoming. May you always know that your voices matter, your hearts are sacred, and your presence is a gift to this world.

To the Parents of Charlotte and Kodie, Thank you for standing beside your children, never in front of them. For showing them that love does not require conformity, and that protection does not have to mean control. Your advocacy, your gentleness, your unwavering support, these are acts of quiet revolution. You are raising children who know their worth and their rights, and in doing so, you are reshaping the meaning of parenting with integrity, presence, and courage.

To My Daughter Kalan, My Greatest Teacher. From the moment you came into my life, you invited me to see through a wider lens. You challenged me to question not only the systems around me, but the beliefs within me. Even as a child, you held an ancient kind of knowing, asking questions no one else dared to ask, offering reflections that pierced through generational silence. You have been my mirror, my guide, and my reminder that love must keep evolving. Your strength has softened me. Your insight has awakened me. And your presence has pushed me to become more than I ever imagined I could be. This work, this book, this healing, it is born from the light you brought into my world.

To all children and educators, I have had the honor of walking beside you over the years. This book is dedicated to you. Your stories, your struggles, and your sacred strengths are the heartbeat of every page. You are the living proof that transformation is not only possible, it is already happening.

Introduction

A Journey Through the Roots That Shaped Us

For over 30 years, I have served as a teacher, leader, and advocate in the field of early childhood education. I have walked alongside children, families, and educators in homes, classrooms, district programs, and private schools, within communities ranging from affluent suburbs to shelters supporting families experiencing homelessness. I've helped teachers discover their strengths, mentored new leaders, and guided programs through accreditation and growth. Through it all, one truth has become crystal clear: How we were raised and trained shapes how we raise and teach others until we choose to rewrite it.

This book was born from that understanding. Roots Rewritten is a reflection of both my personal journey and professional experience. It blends what I've learned about human development, emotional safety, co-regulation, and conscious teaching with real stories from the classroom and home. It is an invitation to pause, reflect, and reconsider the messages we've inherited, because we are not only teaching children, we are carrying forward legacies. Some of those legacies need to be honored. Others need to be questioned. And some... need to be lovingly released.

I still remember standing at the back of a classroom, watching a young boy curl up beneath a table after being scolded for refusing to join circle time. The teacher thought he was being defiant, but I saw something else. I saw a child overwhelmed, unseen, unsure how to belong at that moment. I knelt down, met him where he was, and simply said, "You're safe. I'll sit here with you."

It was one of those small, quiet moments that reminded me: connection must always come before correction.

That's when I knew this work isn't just about children. It's about us. It's about how we carry our own childhood stories into the ways we discipline, nurture, lead, and respond. It's about unlearning the patterns that no longer serve us and embracing new ways of being, rooted in empathy, awareness, and trust.

The child under the table was not the first to reveal this truth to me, and he won't be the last. Again and again, I've witnessed how a single moment of presence can begin to rewrite a story for a child, and for the adult beside them. We are not just shaping behavior, we are shaping belonging. The way we respond matters, and it leaves an imprint that lasts far beyond the classroom or the kitchen table.

Purpose of This Book

In these pages, you will find a balance of research, real-world application, and gentle reflection. I draw on trusted frameworks, including Positive Discipline, Powerful Interactions, and the Developmentally Appropriate Practice (DAP) guidelines from the National Association for the Education of Young Children

(NAEYC). These practices have shaped how I lead, teach, and coach, and they are woven into every chapter that follows.

If you have ever felt a pull to teach or parent differently, to break cycles rather than repeat them, this book is for you. Whether you're a teacher, a parent, a coach, or a leader, I hope these words offer encouragement and insight. May they help you slow down, listen more deeply, and lead with compassion and clarity.

This is not about being perfect; it's about becoming more conscious. And with every shift we make, we create new patterns for the next generation. So let us begin where all rewriting must begin: with the story we were given, with the inheritance we didn't ask for.

Praise for Roots Rewritten
The Story Beneath the Story

"What happens inside the walls, stays inside the walls"? Not exactly. This book knocks gently on those walls and tries to whisper—You are home, my dear. No need to fear."

I met Debbie while working in one of Stanford's ECE programs, where she was my supervisor. Her words in this book echo the same warmth and courage she brought to every classroom she taught in.
—Vandana Laal, M.A. in Human Development, Early Childhood Educator, Leader, and Lifelong Advocate

"Working with Ms. Debbie was a great honor."

She was not just my supervisor; she became a wise friend and mentor. I saw her solve many students' problems with calmness and intelligence. She never shouted or got angry. Instead, she sat quietly with students, listened to their feelings, and helped them find peaceful solutions. What I learned from her was not only about teaching, but also about life. As a mother of two boys, her advice taught me how to turn family difficulties into moments to grow closer. Whenever I felt stuck, I knew I could ask her for help. She always answered with patience and care, never judging. Ms. Debbie is a special person: kind, experienced, and full of wisdom. Learning from her changed how I work, parent, and live. —Junyan (Celia) Meng, Educator, Parent, and Lifelong Advocate

"Debbie is the co-regulation whisperer."

Reading Chapter 11 brought me right back to the time Debbie and I spent together in the after-school program at the school district where we worked. She was my program specialist, and I vividly remember watching her meet a group of challenging fourth-grade girls exactly where they were. She acknowledged their feelings, listened deeply, and reflected with them in a way that helped shift their energy from exclusion to inclusion, from resistance to cooperation. Before long, they were excited to show up, eager to help, and even volunteered to make snacks for the whole group.

What's even more remarkable is that Debbie brought this same gift of co-regulation to us as adults. As teachers and directors, we felt the same way. I remember coming to her, overwhelmed with frustration, and instead of judging me, she offered presence. She helped me calm down, see from the child's or parent's perspective, and grow. Debbie always protected my emotional safety, and because of that, I became a better teacher and director. —Claudia Lopez, Early Childhood and School-Age Educator, Special Education Teacher and Leader

"Reading Roots Rewritten has been a powerful and heartfelt experience."

I've read a few chapters and have truly enjoyed each one. The personal stories are relatable and meaningful, and the classroom examples bring the concepts to life practically and thoughtfully. The authors Debbie references throughout the book add depth, and the poems woven into the text are a beautiful and inspiring touch. Chapter 11, which focuses on co-regulation, stood out as especially impactful, a topic that is so vital and often overlooked. It was one of my favorite chapters. This book is not only informative, it's transformative. I would purchase a copy and recommend it to others. Debbie should be incredibly proud of what she's created. I'm deeply honored to have had the opportunity to read it. —Trish Estelita, Early Childhood Educator and Lifelong Advocate

"Roots Rewritten reminded me that I am not alone."

In the process of transforming how I teach, parent, and lead. This book has helped me reflect on the beliefs I once considered foundational and encouraged me to establish new, conscious roots grounded in connection, awareness, and growth. I wholeheartedly endorse Roots Rewritten as a powerful tool and springboard for anyone seeking to create meaningful change and pursue excellence through heart-centered action. — Dr. Marsha Drew-Harris, Early Childhood Educator, Leader, and Lifelong Advocate

"Fifteen years of knowing Debbie, and still in awe of the way she uplifts others."

I met Debbie 15 years ago, and in that time, I've come to know her as one of the kindest, most thoughtful people I've ever met. She has a way of showing up for others with quiet strength, deep compassion, and a steady belief in people. Her writing reflects that same heart. Roots Rewritten isn't just a book; it's a mirror of how she lives her life: with purpose, with love, and with a genuine desire to help others grow. I'm proud of her, and I believe anyone who reads this will walk away better for it. — Bill Butler, Parent

"One of the biggest lessons I've learned from Debbie is actually about leading adults."

I had the pleasure of working with Debbie at a private preschool. She provided me with a better understanding of children's behaviors and how specific opportunities can be utilized as learning activities. If one child had such big emotions and questions, it's likely that others did too. Understanding the root of a child's behaviors also helps with understanding the roots of adult behaviors. One of the biggest lessons I've learned from Debbie is actually about leading adults: "Find their strength and figure out how you can use that to empower your teachers." This approach has not only helped me develop leaders but also improved morale. I'm excited about her book. I believe with "seen" adults come "seen" children. — Shanda Hendrichs, Early Childhood Educator, Leader, and Lifelong Advocate

"I enjoyed reading Roots as it encourages us to reflect on the trauma we inherit."

I had the pleasure of meeting Debbie, my supervisor, at one of Stanford's early education centers. From our very first encounter, I felt Debbie's warmth and genuine understanding, which quickly turned our professional relationship into a cherished friendship. Her guidance and profound knowledge of child development enriched our center, fostering a supportive atmosphere where both we, as educators, and the children could thrive. I enjoyed reading Roots as it encourages us to reflect on the trauma we inherit and the deep-seated beliefs that shape our actions and perspectives. Debbie went beyond merely outlining the challenges of trauma; she emphasizes the necessity of personal change as a pathway to rewriting our legacies. — Andrea Gonzalez, Early Childhood Educator and Lifelong Advocate

"Debbie never just led from the front."

Debbie listened, noticed the small things, and made you feel like your voice mattered. Her passion for students was evident in everything she did, and as a teacher under her supervision, I felt her support in ways that stayed with me. This book reflects the rare kind of wisdom she brought into every room." –Christy Choi, Educator and Parent.

"Debbie's voice calls on all of us to reflect."

Interestingly, I met Debbie at a time when I was embarking on a new journey, branching out from everything I had lived and breathed while working for a provider for many years. I found myself sitting at a table in a conference room of a car wash, seated across from her. Little did we know, we were both hired for the same position as Center Director at the exact center location. Debbie ended up doing something much, much bigger. That shift gave me the privilege of watching her in action, guiding children with the gentlest of approaches, speaking softly, and bringing a calming presence that's hard to put into words. She nurtured not only children but also teachers and families with incredible grace. In a short time, she became my early childhood sister, a good friend, and colleague. Our paths have remained intertwined ever since as we continue fighting the good fight: to make an impact, to inspire, and to lead teams of educators who hold the future in their hands through the tiniest of humans. As I read through her book, with every page I turned, I could feel Debbie's love and light. Her words echo and call on us to examine our Early Childhood practices, the classroom cultures we create, and the energy we bring into those spaces. She clearly shows that there is another way. –Stacy Gilani, Early Childhood Educator, Leader, and Lifelong Advocate

Table of Contents

Rewriting the Legacy for the Next Generation

Part One: The Past We Must Release

Chapter One – The Inheritance We Didn't Ask For

Chapter Two – The Silence Between Generations

Chapter Three – You Can Love Them and Still Choose a Different Way

Chapter Four – From Survival Parenting to Intentional Parenting

Part Two: The Heart of the Child

Chapter Five – Every Child Is Speaking: Are We Listening?

Chapter Six – Building the Bridge: Emotional Safety First

Chapter Seven – Boundaries Without Shame

Chapter Eight – Honoring the Inner World of the Child

Part Three: The Academic Journey

Chapter Nine – Beyond Grades and Standards

Chapter Ten – Teaching with Purpose and Presence

Chapter Eleven – Co-Regulation in the Classroom

Chapter Twelve – The Whole Child, The Whole Future

Afterward

References

About the Author

Chapter One
The Inheritance We Didn't Ask For

"We are born carrying stories that are not our own. Yet they shape us just the same." ~Debbie Hogue

It all started over a cookie. That's what broke the cycle. I had already told my four-year-old daughter three times that she couldn't have a cookie yet. But she kept going back to the dining room table, reaching for the jar. Each time I said no, she tested the boundary again.

I was determined to teach her that "no" meant "no." I didn't move things out of her reach. I believed she needed to learn discipline—even if that meant consequences—when she wanted something she couldn't have.

So when she screamed for a cookie yet again, I told her no and picked up the belt. That's what my parents did when I didn't listen. She was little, angry, and pushing back. And I stood there, belt in hand, ready to do what I thought was right, what had been done to me in the name of love and obedience.

I started using the belt, convinced I was being firm and consistent. But then my daughter looked at me. In her eyes, I saw something that stopped me cold. She wasn't afraid. She wasn't yielding. She had decided she would let me beat her before giving in.

And in that instant, I saw myself. I saw the same fire I had carried in my own eyes as a child—not defiance, but rebellion. A quiet, fierce resistance that said, "This isn't right."

I realized she was about to be punished, not for stealing or hurting anyone, but for wanting a cookie and not giving up quickly enough. I dropped the belt and, without saying a word, walked into the kitchen and put the cookie jar out of reach. I still held the boundary, but I let go of the violence.

That moment changed everything. It became the beginning of my healing—the first time I chose to parent both the child in front of me and the child I once was. "This isn't just theory—it's lived experience. This is when Roots Rewritten began..."

The Legacy We Carry

Before we speak our first word, we're born into a story already in progress. Our families pass down more than names or features—they pass down ways of being. Some of what we inherit is full of strength and wisdom. But some of it carries wounds that were never acknowledged or healed.

We absorb these legacies long before we can understand them. They show up in how we speak to children, how we interpret emotions, and what we believe about obedience, worth, and love. Many of us learned that compliance meant safety and that "good" children were quiet children.

This inheritance shapes not only our childhoods, but also how we parent and teach. Unless we pause to examine the beliefs we were raised with, we risk passing them on unchanged.

The Patterns We Carry

Some of us grew up learning to follow rules out of fear rather than understanding. We were taught to avoid punishment more than we were encouraged to believe in ourselves. Compliance was expected, but true connection—and the sense of belonging it brings—was often missing.

As a result, we grew up carrying invisible burdens: guilt for asking questions, shame for needing support, fear of failure, and confusion about our worth.

But here's the truth: you can love your parents and still choose a different way. You can honor their sacrifices without repeating their patterns. You can carry forward what was good and gently release what no longer serves.

This book is about that choice. About standing at the crossroads and saying, "The cycle ends with me."

Personal Reflection

I was raised in the Southern Baptist tradition in the deeply conservative state of Texas. Born during the Jones generation—a bridge between the Baby Boomers and Gen X—I grew up in a time marked by shifting cultural values and rising skepticism of authority. I was an outgoing child, constantly pushing boundaries and questioning rules. Like many of my generation, I was taught that discipline and love were often the same. The biblical phrase, "Spare the rod, spoil the child," was not a metaphor; it was a mandate.

I remember one night in elementary school. The rule was clear: be home before the streetlights came on. But I was caught up in play and lost track of time. When I finally got home, my mother was furious. I talked back. The belt came out, leaving bruises behind.

The next morning, I chose the shortest dress I could find. When my mother saw me, I asked, "What do I tell my teacher when she sees my bruises?" Without hesitation, she said, "Tell her you sassed your mother, and she spanked you." Sure enough, my teacher asked. I told her, and she laughed.

At that moment, the seed of rebellion was planted. I didn't feel heard or safe. Instead, I learned to hide the parts of myself that might trigger discipline.

The Power of Conversation

Years later, in eighth grade, I started skipping school. When I got caught, my father did something different. He took me to a small burger joint on Lake Austin. We sat together calmly. No yelling. No belt. Just a conversation. He asked why I did it, and we agreed that I wouldn't skip school again.

Not long after, my friends tried to get me to skip again. I went with them briefly, but the promise I had made to my dad tugged at me. I turned around and headed back. That's when I got caught—returning to school.

This time, the calm was gone. My father didn't ask questions. The belt came out. Grounding began. He said, "I guess that didn't work."

What he didn't realize was that it had worked. I was trying to do the right thing. I just needed the chance to be heard.

The Power of Connection

What I've come to learn—through both life and research—is this: children don't need to be "fixed." They need to be understood.

Modern neuroscience and child development research affirm that young children thrive when they are met with consistency, emotional responsiveness, and opportunities for autonomy (NAEYC, 2021).

Studies show that harsh or punitive discipline does not lead to better long-term outcomes. It is associated with increased aggression, anxiety, and an erosion of trust between children and adults (Gershoff, 2013; Afifi et al., 2017). In contrast, warm and responsive communication strengthens emotional resilience and lays the foundation for self-regulation (Siegel & Bryson, 2012).

In developmentally appropriate classrooms and homes, we don't just correct behavior; we seek understanding. Asking reflective questions, such as "What were you hoping would happen?" or "What was going on in your heart when that happened?" invites children to explore self-awareness. These moments engage the part of the brain responsible for empathy, reasoning, and impulse control (Siegel & Bryson, 2012).

Professional Reflection

Years later, while serving as Director of a Christian preschool, I had a moment that reminded me why these practices matter so much.

One morning, a teacher brought a little boy, whom we'll call Joshua, to my office holding a popped playground ball. "He stepped on it and popped it," she said.

Joshua climbed into the chair, shoulders hunched. When I asked what had happened, he covered his face and repeated, "I'm a bad boy."

My heart dropped. I leaned closer and said gently, "Joshua, you are not a bad boy. Things break sometimes. I just want to understand what was going through your mind when it happened." Slowly, he peeked out from behind his hands.

"I was thinking about when Daddy took me to the store for my birthday stuff. There were balloons. I asked my Daddy how the air got into the balloons, and I was still thinking about that. I wanted to know where the air goes when something pops."

At that moment, everything shifted. "Joshua," I said, "you were asking a science question! That's called air velocity." His eyes lit up.

That afternoon, I shared Joshua's insight with the teachers, and the following week, we turned the incident into a hands-on science exploration. The class experimented with balloons, air pressure, and sound. Joshua transformed from "the boy who popped the ball" to the budding scientist who launched a week of discovery.

Breaking the Cycle

We can break the cycle—but it begins with awareness and the courage to choose differently. NAEYC's DAP reminds us that our role is not to fix children, but to support their learning and development in ways that reflect where they are—individually, culturally, and developmentally. That means trading control for connection, shame for empathy, and reaction for reflection.

The past does not bind you. You are not destined to repeat what you inherited. You have the power to rewrite it—with love, presence, and purpose. The children in your life, whether your own or those you influence, do not have to carry the burdens you choose to heal.

Healing doesn't always happen in a single, dramatic moment. More often, it unfolds slowly—a flicker of awareness here, a gentle shift there—that guides you toward a new way of living and loving.

As we close this first chapter, it's clear that healing begins with awareness. But awareness alone isn't enough. We must move from seeing the patterns to rewriting them in how we parent, teach, and lead. In the next chapter, we'll begin exploring what it looks like to put this awareness into action—one choice, one interaction, one child at a time.

Closing Thoughts

The past does not bind you. You are not destined to repeat what you inherited; you have the power to rewrite it—with love, presence, and purpose.

The children in your life, whether your own or those you influence, do not have to carry the burdens you choose to heal. Through education, exposure, and intention, you can begin to see the world differently and release the unhealthy biases and old stories that no longer serve you.

Healing doesn't always happen in a single, dramatic moment. It usually arrives in whispers, not waves. A flicker of awareness here, a gentle shift there, that guides you toward a new way of living and loving. You are the turning point.

Chapter Two

The Silence Between Generations

"Some things are passed down in words. Others in whispers. And some in silence so loud it echoes through generations." ~Debbie Hogue

As we close Chapter One, we begin to see how our personal histories shape the way we show up for the children in our lives. Now, it's time to turn our focus outward.

Chapter Two invites us to look beyond behaviors and milestones to the emotional undercurrents shaping childhood. What do children truly need from us—and what are they inheriting, silently, from the generations before?

We often speak of inheritance in terms of physical traits: eye color, a dimple, a crooked smile. But there is a more powerful legacy passed from generation to generation—our emotional inheritance. These are the patterns of expression and silence that shape how we love, cope, and connect.

This inheritance doesn't live in our DNA. It's carried in the rhythm of a home, the tone of a parent's voice, the comfort offered—or withheld—in hard moments. It's formed not just by the rules we speak aloud, but by those reinforced in silence.

Many of us were taught how to speak, but not how to say what truly matters. We learned to obey, to keep the peace, to swallow questions that made adults uncomfortable. In that silence, family systems were built: unspoken expectations, hidden griefs, and swallowed dreams, tucked neatly out of sight.

Children hear what adults never say. They absorb tone, posture, and tension, drawing conclusions that become lifelong beliefs. This silence is rarely born of malice. More often, it is rooted in pain that was never acknowledged, wounds that were never healed, and truths that were never allowed to surface (Siegel & Bryson, 2012).

Personal Reflection

When I was in fourth grade, I struggled academically. My teacher once called me a "belligerent little socialite." I didn't fully understand what it meant, but the label stayed with me. That same year, my report card was filled with D's.

One night, I remember my father, after having a few drinks, trying to hold me as I cried. I struggled to get away. He looked at me and said, "What am I supposed to tell people? That you're my little D-maker?" Something in me shifted. I didn't feel seen or supported—I felt small. That night marked the beginning of a long emotional distance between us.

Years later, in high school, I tried to bridge the gap. I wore a T-shirt he had given me that read, "I love my daddy. This Advertisement is paid for by him." It was a small, brave attempt to bring humor where my heart still carried hurt.

But it wasn't until my 40s that true healing began. I sat with my father for hours as he shared the trauma of his own childhood—the belt, the labels, the beatings. He told me about marrying my mother at 17, when they were both still children themselves. He apologized and promised the cycle would end with his grandchildren.

That conversation showed me how much silence can shape a family. What we do not speak about, we often recreate. Breaking the pattern requires naming what was never named and allowing ourselves—and our children—to feel something different (Van der Kolk, 2014).

What Wasn't Said

My parents were not emotionally expressive people. Like many in their generation, they believed that providing a home, food, and safety was enough, and to them, that was love. Feelings were rarely discussed unless they erupted in anger or discipline. I was praised when I was strong, quiet, and helpful, but sadness, fear, or frustration were often viewed as weakness or disobedience.

So I learned to internalize. But what we don't express, we store. And what we store eventually leaks out as anxiety, perfectionism, detachment, or rebellion (Maté, 2010). I chose detachment and rebellion.

This emotional silence wasn't unique to my family. Each generation carries its own version. Our grandparents may have lived through wars, economic hardships, or profound loss, and were taught to "push through" and "be grateful." Our parents, shaped by those same values, often saw emotional expression as indulgent or unproductive. Silence became a survival tool.

Now, many of us—especially those drawn to education, healing, or parenting—find ourselves in a different place. We are the bridge—the ones willing to create something new. But being that bridge can feel lonely, especially when the people who hurt us were also the ones who loved us, the only way they knew how.

The Importance of Teaching Emotional Learning

Helping children understand their emotions is not optional; it's foundational for healthy development. According to NAEYC's DAP position statement, young children must feel emotionally safe to explore and learn.

A simple way to begin is by using emotion icons—visual representations of feelings like happy, sad, angry, or frustrated. These tools help children name emotions in themselves and others. This not only reduces behavioral challenges but also builds empathy and self-awareness, cornerstones of emotional intelligence (Goleman, 1995).

Emotional intelligence is the ability to recognize, understand, and manage emotions effectively. Teaching children this skill gives them language for the invisible. It empowers them to express rather than suppress, to reflect rather than react.

And this work doesn't stop in childhood. As adults, emotional intelligence allows us to repair relationships instead of retreat from them, and to model what it means to be both human and healthy (Siegel, 2020).

Professional Reflection

In my years as a preschool teacher and director, I've seen silence play out in small but powerful ways. One little girl, Ella, used to cry softly in the corner each morning at drop-off. She didn't scream or have a tantrum; she folded inward, clutching a stuffed bunny as if it could hold the tears she wouldn't let fall.

Her teachers assumed she was shy and just needed time to adjust. But something in me whispered, There's more beneath the surface.

One morning, I sat beside her. After a few quiet minutes, I asked gently, "What does your bunny know that you haven't told anyone yet?"

She looked at me for a long time, then whispered, "Sometimes when I cry, Mommy says, 'You're fine. Stop it.'"

That was all she said. But that was everything. Ella wasn't simply sad about saying goodbye; she was learning that her feelings were inconvenient. That silence was safer than expression.

From Silence to Safety

Breaking emotional silence doesn't mean blaming the past. It means creating something new in the present—spaces where feelings are welcome and emotional truth is not only tolerated, but honored.

It can begin with the simplest of invitations:

- "Tell me more."

- "It's okay to feel that way."

- "You don't have to hide your feelings here."

- "What do you need right now?"

These words may seem small, but they are the undoing of shame and the beginning of safety.

There is a silence that lives in many of us—a quiet place where feelings once felt too big or inconvenient to express. As children, we learned that acceptance came when we were "good," "quiet," or "easy to handle." So we tucked away sadness, anger, and confusion, protecting the peace at the cost of our own voice.

When we choose to break that silence—with compassion, not blame—we begin to rewrite the story. One gentle conversation at a time, we show our children and ourselves that emotional truth is not dangerous; it's the doorway to connection.

Closing Thoughts

Silence is never neutral. It shapes the way we love, trust, and teach. But every time you listen—really listen—you change the story.

Every time you invite a child's truth instead of silencing it, you build a new inheritance. You are not just raising children; you are raising a new emotional language, one that heals generations.

Chapter Three

You Can Love Them and Still Choose a Different Way

"You can hold love in your heart and still walk your own path."
~Debbie Hogue

In Chapter Two, we explored how silence shapes families and classrooms in ways that often go unspoken. But awareness is only the beginning. Once we begin to see the patterns we've inherited, the next challenge emerges: the guilt of choosing differently.

Many of us fear that questioning how we were raised means dishonoring those who raised us. But questioning isn't rejection—it's evolution. It's learning to love our parents and teachers for all they gave us, while also being honest about what hurt and what needs to change.

This chapter is about reclaiming the courage to parent, teach, and lead in ways that align with our values, even when it means letting go of deeply ingrained traditions. It's about the tension between honoring our roots and planting something new.

The Courage to Choose Differently

You can love your parents and still choose a different way. You can honor their sacrifices without repeating their patterns. You can carry forward what was good and loving while leaving behind what no longer serves.

Loving your parents while rejecting parts of their parenting model is one of the most courageous acts a person can take. It's the tender place between gratitude and growth, the space where healing lives.

Many of us carry guilt for wanting to do things differently. We fear that naming the harm we experienced will be seen as a betrayal. But questioning is not condemnation; it's evolution. To love someone deeply and still say, "This part hurt," or "This won't continue through me," is a sign of strength, not disloyalty (Brown, 2010).

Because you can love them and still let go. Because you can honor your roots and still grow in a new direction. Healing doesn't mean turning away from your family; it means turning toward the future with love, clarity, and intention (Maté, 2010).

You are not failing them. You are freeing yourself. And in doing so, you are freeing future generations.

Personal Reflection

I grew up in a privileged environment. From the outside, our life looked stable, even enviable—big family meals, holiday traditions, and a strong sense of pride in where we came from. But beneath that surface was a story that shaped a huge part of who I am today. It wasn't just about material comfort or social standing. It was about the unspoken rules, the emotional silence, and the deeply rooted beliefs passed down like heirlooms.

In my family, emotions were often tucked away, appearances mattered, and questioning the way things were done wasn't encouraged. I learned early how to read a room, how to shrink parts of myself to maintain peace, and how to carry burdens I didn't fully understand. That's the thing about inherited stories: they're not always spoken aloud, but they live in the way we communicate, love, discipline, and cope.

In this silence, I learned a painful lesson at a very young age. My family hired a housekeeper, a woman of color, who worked in our home for many years. Her daughter, who was my age, played with me every day. To me, she was simply my friend. We laughed, ran, and shared the innocence of childhood.

One day, around age five, I asked my mother if my friend could spend the night. She paused and then explained, "Their culture and ours have separate places in society." She didn't say it with anger—only as if passing along a rule she didn't write, only followed.

I didn't understand. I only knew it felt wrong. Why could we share daylight but not moonlight? Why were there invisible lines I wasn't allowed to cross with someone I loved?

Another memory from that same era still burns in my chest: the day my mother and our neighbors argued loudly about desegregation busing. I didn't fully understand what was happening, but I felt the fear and anger in their voices. They spoke of "those children from the wrong side of the tracks" as if they were a threat.

Desegregation busing in the 1960s and 1970s was meant to integrate schools following Brown v. Board of Education (1954), but it was met with resistance in many white communities. That day, I saw how prejudice didn't always sound cruel; it could be cloaked in "protection," "community values," and fear disguised as love.

As an adult, I now understand what I witnessed: deeply rooted racial and cultural divides passed down from one generation to the next, often without question and embedded in "the way things are" (DiAngelo, 2018). And these inherited norms still surface in education today:

- Miscommunications between staff and families due to cultural or religious expectations

- Conflicting views on discipline or emotional expression

- Struggles between upholding school policy and respecting home values

These are not abstract debates. They are lived tensions, weighted by history and silence.

As a child, I couldn't make sense of those rules. As an adult, I've made it my mission to question them. Children deserve spaces where they don't have to choose between love and belonging. We must stop reenacting old systems of power under the name of tradition.

We can honor our families while acknowledging where they were wrong. We can love those who raised us while teaching something new to those we raise. As educators and parents, it's our responsibility to challenge these inherited messages about power and belonging so that the children in our care can grow up in spaces where love and belonging are never at odds.

From Silence to Conscious Choice

It took years to unlearn the bias I absorbed. I grew up during the Civil Rights Movement. I remember the grief of Martin Luther King Jr.'s assassination, the hush in adult voices, the fear woven into closed-door conversations.

At the time, I thought that fear was the truth. It was the air I breathed. It wasn't until much later—through honest reflection, listening, and learning—that I understood how much of what I had inherited wasn't mine to keep.

Naming it allowed me to change. Challenging it allowed me to teach differently. Letting go allowed me to love more freely. That is the work of this chapter: to recognize what we've been handed and choose, consciously, what we will pass on.

Professional Reflection

When I first entered the preschool classroom as a teacher at age 28, I was idealistic and eager. My co-teacher, 15 years my senior, was a seasoned educator I admired. Early in the year, a joyful child of color joined our class. While preparing the new student's cubby, my co-teacher smiled and said, "I'm so excited she's joining us. I always wanted a little Black rag doll."

Her words froze me. She didn't mean harm. It was an inherited belief she had never examined. I didn't know what to say. I was young. I stayed silent.

Years later, I understand why it struck me: children are not dolls. They are not here for our comfort or curiosity. They are whole people who deserve deep respect.

This story isn't about blame. It's about pattern recognition. I've heard similar phrases in classrooms:

- "You know how they are."

- "That's part of their culture."

- "He's one of those kids."

Even when well-intended, these labels limit children. They reduce them to stereotypes and teach others to view them through assumptions.

Bias doesn't always sound cruel. Sometimes it sounds kind. That's why we must keep doing the work—to go beyond cultural awareness into cultural humility and human awareness (Hammond, 2015).

The Hidden Curriculum

Bias in classrooms often lives in the unnoticed spaces—in what we don't say, what we assume, and what we allow. It's not always loud; in fact, it's usually polite, invisible to those who aren't impacted.

This is called the hidden curriculum: the unwritten, unofficial, and often unintended lessons that shape a child's sense of identity and belonging (Nieto, 2010). It shows up in:

- Which books do we read, and whose stories do we prioritize
- How holidays are celebrated
- Which hairstyles are labeled as "messy"
- Which emotions are quickly redirected or silenced

Consider these examples:

- A Black child is praised for sitting quietly, while a white child is celebrated for being outspoken.
- A Latinx family is reminded more often than others about "bringing snacks on time."
- An Asian child's shyness is labeled as "not participating," instead of being honored as a temperament.

These small moments add up. They shape how children see themselves and how they believe the world sees them.

Our Purpose With Children and Families

Working with children and families is more than a job; it's a responsibility. It's not just about ratios, lesson plans, or behavior charts. It's about entering lives with compassion and choosing to see the whole child—their history, heartbreaks, and hope—and offering something steady in a world that often asks them to shrink.

To work with families is to stand at the intersection of generations: past, present, and future. You become a translator of stories, a pattern-breaker, a mirror that reflects not just who a child is, but who they are becoming.

Our role is not to replicate the past uncritically. It is to honor what was beautiful—cultural values, strength, and resilience born from adversity—while releasing what was rooted in fear, shame, or unconscious bias. We do this not out of judgment, but out of reverence for what's possible.

Letting go of inherited teachings is not a sign of disrespect; it's a matter of integrity. It takes strength to say, "This was given to me with love, but I choose to carry it differently." It takes wisdom to see that love and harm can exist in the same story, and even more courage to rewrite the ending.

A Call to Courage

If we are serious about raising conscious children, we must also be serious about doing our own work. That means:

- Attending anti-bias and anti-racism trainings

- Building diverse libraries that reflect the world, not just our bubble

- Reflecting on our own conditioning, even when it's uncomfortable

- Listening deeply to the voices of families and children whose lives differ from our own

- Speaking up when we hear subtle or overt harm

Silence is not neutrality; it's complicity. And children are always listening. As educators and parents, we are co-creating the future.

Closing Thoughts

We were not born to repeat. We were born to remember, reimagine, and rise. Each time we choose awareness over autopilot, presence over pressure, and truth over tradition, we heal.

You are not just teaching children. You are teaching a new way to be human, and that changes everything.

Chapter Four

From Survival Parenting To Intentional Parenting

"We feared the belt because we were never invited to trust the voice that held it." ~Debbie Hogue

In Chapter Three, we explored how guilt can surface when we decide to do things differently than those who raised us. But choosing a new way forward isn't only about honoring our values—it's also about understanding the patterns we've inherited and how deeply they shape the way we parent, teach, and lead. These patterns can feel automatic, woven into our responses before we even realize it.

This chapter is about moving from survival-based parenting—the parenting many of us grew up with—to intentional parenting, where connection, respect, and presence guide the way. It's about slowing down enough to notice the habits we've carried forward, asking where they came from, and choosing whether they still serve the child in front of us.

The Legacy of Survival Parenting

Many of us were parented from a place of survival, where fear was the motivator, control was the method, and obedience was the goal. Survival parenting was shaped by the belief that safety came through submission and that love had to be earned by being "good."

In households shaped by this philosophy, love often felt conditional—dependent on behavior, achievement, or silence (Brown, 2010). Survival parenting often sounded like:

- "Because I said so."

- "Stop crying or I'll give you something to cry about."

- "Good kids don't act like that."

- "You need to toughen up."

- "Boys don't cry."

- "You're being too sensitive."

These messages weren't always delivered with malice. Often, they came from exhaustion, desperation, or a deeply rooted belief that this was the only way to raise a respectful child. Many of our parents or grandparents carried their own unhealed wounds and repeated what they were taught, never given the tools or space to question it (Van der Kolk, 2014).

Regardless of intent, these messages echoed through our childhoods like quiet thunder, leaving many of us feeling unseen, unheard, and unsafe in our own emotional skin.

Healing Over Harm

Fear-based parenting may have been necessary for survival in times of instability, poverty, war, or cultural oppression, but we are no longer bound to those conditions. We are the bridge between the past and the future. And now, with greater awareness, we can make different choices:

- Healing over harm
- Connection over control
- Presence over performance

Intentional parenting is not about perfection. It's about conscious parenting rooted in presence, attunement, and mutual respect. This approach aligns with NAEYC's (2020) emphasis on developmentally appropriate practice, which calls for culturally responsive, relationship-based interactions tailored to each child's needs and context.

Intentional parenting begins by asking, "What does my child need at this moment?" instead of "How do I make them stop?" It's a shift:

- From reacting to responding
- From managing behavior to nurturing the child behind the

behavior

- From fear to trust

Intentional parenting sounds like:

- "I want to understand what you're feeling."

- "You're safe here, even with big emotions."

- "We can figure this out together."

- "Your voice matters."

- "I'm here, even when it's hard."

This approach is not permissive. It holds boundaries, but those boundaries are built with empathy and guided by respect, rather than punishment. It understands that discipline is meant to teach, not to shame, and that our role is not to break a child's will but to guide their spirit (Kennedy, 2022).

Healing the Child Within

When we shift from survival-based patterns to intentional parenting, we don't just raise emotionally whole children—we reparent ourselves.

We begin to soften the inner voice that once echoed, "Be quiet. Be good. Don't feel too much." In its place, we nurture a voice of self-compassion:

- "It's okay to feel, to need, to be human."

- "You were doing your best with what you knew."

- "You deserved gentleness, even when you didn't receive it."

- "You are worthy of love without performance."

This is the essence of reparenting: to offer ourselves the kindness and understanding we may have longed for as children.

This chapter is not about blame. It's about breaking the cycle of silence, fear, and inherited patterns that no longer serve us. It's about honoring the lineage we came from while courageously evolving it into something more compassionate and connected.

Just as a tree grows toward the light, we, too, can reach for something new while still rooted in where we came from.

Personal Reflection

As I shared in Chapter Three, I grew up surrounded by subtle but firm cultural biases from a young age. I didn't have the language or awareness to question it—it was simply "the way things were."

One of the earliest moments that began to shift my perspective occurred during my young adulthood. I watched a movie about a man of color and a white woman falling in love. Something stirred inside me. I remember thinking, "Love is love; who are we to stand in its way?" But even then, I clung to an old belief that they shouldn't have children because it "wouldn't be fair" to the child. That belief was rooted not in love but in fear.

When I moved to California, my world opened. I worked with families from every background—blended, international, interfaith, interracial. I witnessed both the beauty and complexity of their lives. Something in me softened again. I began to understand that there is no difference between my life and theirs. Love is love. Family is family.

Then, fifteen years ago, I met the man who would become my life partner, a man of color. My hesitation wasn't about how I felt about him; it was about the fear of what he might endure and how my family might respond. He lovingly called me out and said, "That's a cop-out." He was right.

When I told my father who I was dating, we were sitting in an airport. He literally fell out of his chair. That moment marked not just discomfort but a line between who I had been and who I was becoming.

Healing, I've learned, doesn't always look like a lightning bolt. Sometimes it's a slow burn—like the quiet unfolding of clarity after years of confusion.

Education and exposure are key to this process. They help us see beyond old narratives and challenge unhealthy biases we may have carried unknowingly. If you're reading this and finding pieces of your own story in mine, know this: healing often meets us not with thunder, but with a flicker. And that flicker is enough to light the way forward—a step-by-step unraveling of old stories and a choosing, again and again, to live by a more profound truth.

This Is Generational Work

When we shift from survival parenting to intentional parenting, we aren't just changing routines—we are transforming legacies.

Survival parenting taught us how to get through, but rarely how to connect. It treated emotions as threats and behavior as disobedience. Many of us grew up disconnected from our inner world because our caregivers didn't know how to see it.

But what if we said, "The pain stops here"? What if we chose:

- "This doesn't feel right in my body, and I'm allowed to choose another way."

- "I don't have to use shame to teach."

- "Connection is more powerful than correction."

This is not about perfection. It's about presence. It's about waking up to our automatic reactions and becoming curious about the beliefs behind them.

Professional Reflection

As teachers, we often find ourselves at the intersection of differing beliefs, not just between children and adults but also between families and schools.

One of the most common tensions arises when a parent expects the teacher to "spoon-feed" their child, not out of neglect, but because, in their culture, interdependence is often seen as a sign of love (Rogoff, 2003).

In many collectivist cultures, anticipating your child's needs, doing things for them, and staying physically close are expressions of love. In contrast, Western early childhood philosophy often champions independence and problem-solving.

This cultural difference can be challenging in classrooms with eight to twelve children and limited staff. But the solution isn't to choose one over the other—it's to find a bridge:

- Start with empathy: "Can you tell me what independence looks like at home?"

- Explain the 'why': "We support self-help skills to build confidence and resilience."

- Find a middle ground: "We'll model the task and support your child as they try it."

- Reinforce connection: "This isn't about rejecting your family's values; it's about preparing your child to thrive in a group setting with care and respect."

According to NAEYC (2020), high-quality early childhood practice requires teachers to integrate children's social, cultural, and linguistic contexts into every decision. Honoring cultural differences while teaching universal life skills is the heart of intentional, inclusive education.

When children feel seen and supported at home and school, they thrive.

This Work Is Important

Intentional parenting means we hold the emotional map for our children, even as we tape back together the torn pages of our own. Each meltdown is not just a call to soothe our child, but also an invitation to cradle the wounded child within ourselves.

Every time we validate a child's emotions, we send healing backward through time. We whisper to our lineage:

- "You didn't have this, but your descendants will."
- "You weren't allowed to feel, but we feel now."
- "You were silenced, but we will speak and we will listen."

When we choose empathy over enforcement, we build homes where children are not afraid to be themselves. We raise whole, resilient, deeply connected humans. And we become one, too.

Closing Thoughts

Cultural understanding is not about choosing sides; it's about building bridges. When we lead with respect, listen with openness, and teach with flexibility, we create classrooms and homes where both independence and belonging can thrive.

Every child walks into our care carrying a world of experiences, traditions, and stories. When we take the time to truly see and honor that world, we send a powerful message: You matter. You belong.

This isn't about perfection; it's about presence. It's about asking more questions than we answer, slowing down long enough to hear what is unspoken, and adjusting our practices so all children feel valued.

As educators, parents, and caregivers, we hold an extraordinary opportunity to shape the future, not by molding children into one way of being, but by nurturing their wholeness. When we choose connection over control and curiosity over judgment, we become the bridge between where a child is and all they are capable of becoming.

May we each commit to doing this work with humility and hope, knowing that every moment of genuine understanding plants seeds of peace that will outlive us.

Chapter Five
Every Child Is Speaking: Are We Listening?

*"When children are swept up in big emotions,
they don't need us to match their storm;
they need us to anchor the calm."* ~Debbie Hogue

In Chapter Four, we explored how shifting from survival-based parenting to intentional parenting can transform the way we connect with children. But connection isn't just about how we discipline or set boundaries—it's also about how we listen.

To truly connect, we must learn to slow down. Children's communication is often subtle, layered in glances, tones, and unspoken needs. When we rush through the day, we risk missing the moments that matter most.

Children Speak Long Before Words

Long before a child learns to speak, they are already communicating. Through body language, facial expressions, cries, laughter, and silence, children send messages about their needs, fears, joys, and boundaries.

As adults, we often believe communication begins with language. But for children, especially in their early years, communication begins with connection.

- It's in the glance cast when unsure.

- It's in the tone of a toddler's "no."

- It's in the meltdown that masks overstimulation.

Every behavior is a message. Every emotion is a doorway. Every interaction is a chance to speak into the spirit of a child.

When we pause long enough to truly listen—not just to the words, but to the heart behind them—we begin to understand the unspoken language of childhood. We notice the subtle cues that say, "I need safety." We hear the silence that whispers, "I feel unseen." We recognize that a tantrum isn't defiance but a cry for regulation.

Listening in this way requires slowing down, softening our responses, and shifting from correction to connection. It's choosing curiosity over control and seeing the world through their eyes, even for a moment.

When children feel heard—not just managed—they begin to trust. And trust is the soil in which confidence, empathy, and healthy relationships grow.

CHAPTER FIVE

Personal Reflection

My father used to say, "When God made a Hogue, He broke the mold." That phrase stayed with me. It meant we were one of a kind, maybe even destined for something meaningful. I didn't realize it then, but those words were shaping me long before I had the language to name them.

Growing up, I experienced both ends of the parenting spectrum: punishments, groundings, lectures, and the quiet withdrawal of approval, but also moments of profound affirmation. Words like "You're better than that" and "You can do anything you set your mind to" carried a reverence that made me feel as though something unseen and powerful lived inside me.

Even when I pushed back or made mistakes, a quiet belief began to take root: being a "Hogue" meant I mattered. It gave me a sense of pride, of coming from strong stock, of knowing I could rise, even from hard places.

Now, after years of healing, I've realized it wasn't fear that shaped me. It wasn't discipline that made me strong; it was the belief that I already was. That's what I want to pass on:

- Not praise tied to performance.

- Not love tied to perfection.

- But identity rooted in worthiness—a sense of belonging that doesn't have to be earned.

The words we speak to children become the beliefs they carry. I want every child, whether born into the Hogue line or welcomed into my circle, to know: You are already enough. You don't have to be perfect to be powerful. You don't have to be obedient to be seen. You are not defined by what you do, but by who you are. And who you are is worthy of love.

Language as Identity

Language is one of the most powerful tools we have. It doesn't just shape the world around us—it shapes how children see themselves. A simple phrase like "You're so thoughtful" affirms identity. A careless, "What's wrong with you?" can echo as shame.

Children absorb everything—not just our words, but how we say them. Tone, timing, consistency, and body language are all part of the message.

When we choose language that is intentional, respectful, and rooted in empathy, we tell children:

- You are seen.

- You are valued.

- You are capable.

Many of us were raised on automatic scripts: "Because I said so." "You're being bad." These weren't conscious choices; they were inherited patterns. But here's the truth: we can rewrite them.

When we become conscious of our language, we begin to break cycles. We model self-regulation, emotional literacy, and empathy. When we speak with intention, we're not just managing behavior—we're nurturing identity.

Behavior as Communication

In early childhood education, one of the most foundational truths is this: All behavior is communication.

Dr. Ross Greene reminds us: "Children do well if they can." When they can't, it's not defiance—it's a lack of skill, safety, or regulation (Greene, 2014).

Instead of labeling behavior as "attention-seeking," what if we saw it as "connection-seeking"? This simple shift opens the door to compassion.

According to NAEYC, responsive and respectful communication is a cornerstone of developmentally appropriate practice. Language has a direct influence on a child's self-concept, emotional security, and ability to form trusting relationships.

NAEYC emphasizes: "Teachers foster communication and language development by listening, responding thoughtfully, and using language that is rich, descriptive, and respectful."

Dr. Bruce Perry reminds us that connection begins with presence. When a child is overwhelmed, the first thing they need isn't correction—it's our calm attention. Compassionate phrases like:

- "I see this is hard for you right now."

- "Let's breathe together."

- "I'm here with you."

...become bridges of understanding. They affirm the child's experience and help ground their nervous system, creating the safety from which trust and learning can grow (Perry & Szalavitz, 2021).

Language, the Brain, and the Heart

The prefrontal cortex—the part of the brain responsible for logic and impulse control—continues to develop well into young adulthood. The emotional brain (the limbic system) often leads the way. That's why:

- Shame shuts down learning

- Harshness overrides reasoning

- Connection is the path to correction

Dr. Dan Siegel encourages us to "connect before you correct." Speak to the emotion first. Guide the behavior once the child feels safe (Siegel & Bryson, 2012).

Professional Reflection

There was a child I once worked with—we'll call him Daniel. He had a fire in him, a strong will, and a deep need to be seen. Most teachers struggled with him, especially those who had little patience for the emotional storms he brought with him. Daniel was often labeled "angry" or "defiant," but what I saw was a child who didn't feel heard. His behavior was his protest, a signal flare for connection.

One day, a teacher came into my office to report another incident with Daniel. When she left, another leader whom I deeply respect turned to me and said, "He's just a brat. We need to lay down the law."

Something rose in me, and I responded, more sharply than I usually would: "He's not a brat. No child is. He needs patience. He needs guidance. And most of all, he needs to be heard."

Later, I visited Daniel's classroom and asked the teacher to step outside with him so we could talk together. As soon as we stepped into the hallway, she launched into him: "Everyone in the classroom is scared of you. I'm scared of you."

I leaned my back against the wall and held my tongue in front of Daniel. I didn't want to shame her in the same way she was unintentionally shaming him. But after she returned to class, I asked her to come speak with me privately.

"We do not make children responsible for adult emotions," I said calmly but firmly. "That's not their burden to carry. Telling a child that everyone is afraid of them is not just unkind. It's cruel. Whether or not you believe it's true, it doesn't belong at a child's feet."

She disagreed with me, but I stood my ground. "Our job," I reminded her, "is to help children cope with their emotions, not weaponize those emotions against them. There's not a single adult I know who would want to be treated that way, so why would we think it's okay to do that to a child?"

I knew Daniel needed something different, so I invited him to my office. He didn't walk in; he guarded his way in—shoulders tight, jaw clenched, eyes scanning the room for a fight before a word was even spoken.

I greeted him the same way I always did: with presence, without judgment. "Hey, Daniel. I'm glad you're here." I reminded him he wasn't in trouble. That my office was a safe space. That I was here to listen.

At first, he scowled, arms crossed, heart locked behind walls. I didn't talk to him; I spoke with him. I acknowledged his struggle and invited him into a solution. Together, we made a plan: he would notice his anger before it took over, and we chose a quiet space in the classroom—his space—where he could go to reset.

The next day, he was back. Another outburst. Another child was hurt. His fists were clenched in shame and anger as I knelt beside him.

"Daniel, we're going to have to call home today," I said softly. His shoulders dropped, heavy with defeat.

I paused and added, "My job is to keep everyone safe, including you. Right now, your body needs a break. But this doesn't mean I'm giving up on you. I still believe in you."

As I stood, his small voice caught me: "Ms. Debbie..."

I turned back and met his eyes. "I really think I can do it," he whispered, almost afraid to hope.

I crouched down once more, steady and sure. "I know you can," I said, wanting Daniel to feel the truth in my words.

That moment didn't erase Daniel's struggles. But it was the beginning of something far more critical: his belief. A belief not born from fear or consequence, but from connection—the quiet certainty that someone saw him, believed in him, and would stand by him even when things got hard.

Moments like these remind me that many of us—children and adults alike—are still learning, still unlearning, and still finding the courage to break the cycles we inherited. When we lead with connection instead of control, we change the story for a child. And sometimes, that shift begins not with a grand gesture, but with a single, steady message: You are not too much. You are not alone. And I believe in you.

The Power of Language

Just as children communicate through behavior, we communicate through presence—through tone, timing, and intention. When we:

- Respond with curiosity instead of criticism

- Offer encouragement instead of judgment

- Listen with our whole selves

...we teach children: You matter. Your voice matters. Intentional language creates emotional safety. It transforms correction into connection. It teaches children that their inner world is welcome here.

Identity Through Language

Every word we speak becomes part of a child's inner narrative. Psychologist Carol Dweck found that praising effort over outcome fosters a growth mindset. "You worked so hard on that puzzle," teaches resilience. "You're so smart" can lead to fear of failure (Dweck, 2006). We must understand what drives a child's behavior:

- Internal motivation: the desire to do something simply because it's enjoyable

- External motivation: rewards or punishment

- Intrinsic motivation: a child's natural drive for curiosity and mastery

Too often, we unintentionally replace curiosity with compliance. But language doesn't just describe the world—it defines it. Use it to build equity. Use it to nurture empathy. Use it to reflect worth.

The Power of Repair

We won't always get it right. That's okay. What matters most is that we repair. A simple, "I'm sorry I raised my voice. That must have felt scary," teaches accountability, emotional safety, and the power of apology. These are lessons children carry with them long after they leave our care.

Closing Thoughts

Every child carries a sacred flame. Our job isn't to light it, but to protect it from the wind. When we honor a child's inner world over our need for control, we begin the real work of generational healing. We move from managing behavior to mentoring the child. We become the adults we once needed. And that changes everything.

Chapter Six
Building the Bridge: Emotional Safety First

"Gentle discipline begins with reparenting yourself – rooted in respect, nurtured through relationship, and expressed in a new way of parenting." ~*Debbie Hogue*

In Chapter Five, we explored how listening deeply—beneath the words and behaviors—can transform the way children see themselves and their place in the world. But listening is only part of the equation.

Children also need boundaries, not as battlegrounds, but as bridges. Boundaries that teach, guide, and protect while preserving connection. This chapter is about reimagining discipline and boundaries, not as battlegrounds, but as bridges that connect children to safety, self-worth, and the adults who love them (Siegel & Bryson, 2011).

Reclaiming Discipline

There was a time when the word "discipline" made my stomach tighten. It conjured echoes of cold stares, raised voices, slammed doors, and the aching loneliness that followed. For many of us, discipline was not guidance; it was punishment masked as love, control masked as protection. We learned to fear mistakes rather than grow from them.

But I have come to learn that proper discipline—gentle, respectful, and rooted in relationship—isn't about controlling children. It's about teaching, guiding, and holding space for them to rise into their full humanity, even in moments of chaos or challenge.

And to do that, we must also be willing to hold space for our own inner child. Because the patterns we inherited—the ones that taught us fear, shame, or silence—don't simply vanish when we become adults. They live in our reactions, the tone we use.

What Gentle Discipline Is, and Isn't

There's a common misconception that gentle discipline means being soft, permissive, or passive—that it's about giving children whatever they want or letting them "run the show." But that couldn't be further from the truth.

Gentle discipline is not about being less firm; it's about being more intentional. It is a conscious choice to lead with connection rather than control, and to model emotional regulation rather than demand blind obedience.

At its heart, gentle discipline asks: What is the lesson I want to teach in this moment? It shifts the focus from punishment to partnership, from compliance to growth (Greene, 2016).

Traditional discipline often relies on fear, force, or shame to stop unwanted behavior. Gentle discipline takes a different approach. It looks beneath the surface, viewing behavior as communication—a signal of unmet needs, lagging abilities, or emotional overwhelm that spills into their behavior."

Rather than asking, "How do I stop this behavior?" we begin to ask, "What is this behavior trying to tell me?" (Shanker, 2016).

Gentle discipline does not mean there are no boundaries. In fact, it requires strong and consistent boundaries—but they are set with clarity, kindness, and compassion.

It means saying "no" without yelling. Following through without breaking the connection. And understanding that discipline is not something we do to a child, but something we do with them, side by side, as they grow (Center on the Developing Child, 2015).

The Latin root of "discipline" is disciplina—instruction or knowledge. Yet over the generations, it became distorted, used as a tool for domination and control. Our work now is to reclaim it: to guide rather than punish, to teach rather than shame, and to hold both the child and the boundary with equal care.

The Language of Respect

Words shape worlds. Especially for children, the language we use becomes the lens through which they see themselves. Over time, it becomes the voice they carry within.

Respectful discipline begins not just with what we do, but with what we say and how we say it (Beck, 2001). A loving boundary offered with calm presence can build connection. That same boundary, delivered with sharpness or sarcasm, can chip away at trust.

These are not just semantic changes; they are emotional ones. They model regulation, accountability, and empathy. They preserve a child's sense of self-worth while guiding them back into alignment (Siegel & Hartzell, 2003).

And here's the more profound truth: when we practice speaking to children with respect, we begin to heal the way we talk to ourselves.

The way we discipline often reflects the way we were spoken to—or the way our inner voice still talks to us. But when we pause, breathe, and choose different words, we break the cycle. We don't just raise emotionally resilient children; we raise ourselves, again.

Personal Reflection

I know I've shared many childhood stories throughout this book, but this one rests especially close to my heart because it touches not only my experience but my daughter's as well.

From a young age, I was labeled by teachers, family members, and even those who claimed to love me. I was called a "belligerent little socialite," a "troublemaker," someone who "talked too much" or "thought too highly" of herself. They didn't see a spirited, curious, passionate child—they saw someone who needed to be tamed. Those words stuck.

What hurt even more was watching those same labels passed down to my youngest daughter. "She's just like her mother," they would say. But not with pride. Their tone carried judgment, as if my voice, my strength, my qualities were curses she had inherited.

For years, my daughter rebelled against the idea of being "just like her mother." It was her way of claiming independence and finding her own voice. But as time passed, she began to see the love, strength, and quiet sacrifice that had shaped her childhood.

In tenth grade, she wrote a paper about her journey. She talked about the sting of those labels, the weight of constant comparison, and her fight to define herself on her own terms. Near the end, she wrote the words that moved me to tears: "I am proud to be just like my mother."

That sentence lives in my heart. It reminds me that sometimes the seeds we plant in love take years to bloom, but when they do, the harvest is more beautiful than we ever imagined.

But this story also reveals how generational trauma creeps through families and systems, not always through violence or cruelty, but through language. Through labels. Through the stories, we don't question. The most dangerous part is how normal it can all feel if we don't pause to look closely.

I've looked closely. And I've made a vow: the cycle ends here. We are not our labels. We are not the shame someone else projected onto us. And our children should never be made to carry the weight of our unhealed wounds.

When the old voice creeps in—the one that whispers, "you're too much" or "you're not enough"—I stop and speak a new truth. I say it to myself. I tell it to my daughter. And I say it to every child I've ever had the honor of teaching:

You are not a brat. You are not a problem. You are not too much. You are seen. You are heard. You are becoming. That is the legacy I choose to leave.

Shame Versus Accountability

There is a quiet but powerful difference between shame and accountability—one that determines whether a child grows up feeling empowered to make better choices or burdened by the belief that they are inherently flawed (Neff, 2011).

- Accountability is a healthy skill. In a safe environment, children learn to take ownership of their actions and understand their impact.

- Shame corrodes self-worth.

Shame also breeds anger, rebellion, and detachment—not because children don't care, but because they are protecting themselves from pain. Repeated shame can erode empathy, not as a failure of character, but as a survival adaptation (Perry & Szalavitz, 2006).

Accountability, by contrast, separates the child from the behavior. It reminds them that mistakes are part of learning, not proof of unworthiness.

And perhaps the most powerful shift is the one we make in ourselves: when we stop using shame as a tool of control, we stop replicating the voices we grew up with. We begin to lead from truth, not trauma.

The Lightness of Humor

Sometimes, the message of accountability is best delivered with a bit of lightness. Humor, used with presence and care, can be a powerful tool for connection. A silly face, a gentle exaggeration, or shared laughter can release tension and open the door to communication.

Humor doesn't minimize the moment; it humanizes it. It tells children: "We're okay. We're still connected. We can move through this together."

But humor is not sarcasm. Sarcasm often cloaks judgment or frustration, and for children—especially younger ones—it can feel mocking or cruel. While humor invites closeness, sarcasm creates distance.

When we use playfulness in the classroom or at home, we are not dismissing a child's feelings; we are inviting joy back into the relationship. A well-timed smile or light-hearted comment can transform a power struggle into a moment of mutual understanding.

Professional Reflection

At the beginning of a school year, one of our teachers experienced a family emergency, and I stepped in to cover her Pre-K classroom for seven weeks.

It had been years since I was full-time in the classroom, but I let my playful side lead. I used humor to bring levity to the classroom. At lunch, I'd pretend the ceiling art was whispering secrets to me. On the playground, I joined the children's games with joyful abandon. We laughed a lot.

One child, Arjun, was having a difficult time adjusting. I didn't push or prod. I showed up with presence, consistency, and a bit of silliness. Soon, he became my little shadow.

After I returned to my leadership role, Arjun asked to visit my office each morning before class. Those brief moments of connection anchored him. And it wasn't just him—other children began greeting me with the same excitement. Humor built trust. Playfulness rooted in love created safety.

The Legacy We Choose to End

For generations, discipline was carried forward through lineage: rigid, fear-based, rooted in control. Many of us were raised in homes where love was withdrawn when we made mistakes, where boundaries were laced with shame, and where obedience was valued over understanding.

But we are not bound to repeat what we lived through. The legacy we choose to end is not just about how we treat children; it's about how we treat ourselves. Every pause, every repair, every moment of presence is a quiet revolution. We prove to ourselves and to our children: it can be different.

As Dr. Gabor Maté (2019) reminds us, the emotional wounds we carry—often inherited unconsciously—become the framework through which we relate to others, especially children. Healing begins when we recognize these patterns and choose to respond differently: with compassion instead of control, presence instead of power.

Closing Thoughts

There is no such thing as a perfect parent, teacher, or leader. But there is such a thing as a present one.

- Each time you pause before reacting...

- Each time you choose empathy over power...

You are not only helping a child; you are healing a pattern. It's okay to feel uncomfortable as you rewrite what was once familiar. That discomfort is not failure—it's transformation. Remember, you are not just raising a child. You are raising a person. You are raising a legacy.

Let this be the chapter where the cycle ends, where the bridge begins, and where we raise the next generation with dignity, strength, and a deep sense of belonging.

Chapter Seven

Boundaries Without Shame

"Discipline, when redefined through dignity and love, becomes a path to connection, not control."
~Debbie Hogue

In Chapter Six, we explored how boundaries can become bridges—spaces where connection and guidance work together. But too often, boundaries have been paired with shame, used as tools to control rather than teach.

This chapter is about letting go of that belief and reclaiming discipline as a practice of teaching, not punishing. It's about choosing boundaries that teach safety and self-worth, that help children rise rather than shrink. When we lead with respect and compassion, we create spaces where children not only follow rules but also understand why they matter.

The Myth of Shame

For generations, we believed that shame was a necessary tool to mold character. We thought that making children feel small would somehow make them grow. We believed fear would create respect, humiliation would build humility, and guilt would lead to goodness. But shame does not teach belonging; it teaches unworthiness (Brown, 2010).

When a child internalizes shame, they don't separate behavior from identity. Instead of thinking, "I made a mistake," they begin to believe, "I am a mistake." Rather than feeling safe to grow, they become afraid to be seen. This deep sense of "something is wrong with me" can linger into adulthood, showing up as self-doubt, self-sabotage, perfectionism, anxiety, and anger. Ironically, the behaviors we try to "fix" through shame often become more deeply rooted, just hidden from view.

Boundaries Aren't the Problem

The myth was never that boundaries are bad. Boundaries are essential. The myth was that shame was the way to protect them. Actual boundaries do not rely on humiliation. Instead, they stand in quiet strength: firm, kind, unwavering. They say:

- "This is the line, because love lives inside these lines."

- "You are safe here."

- "You are worthy, even when you make mistakes."

It's time to retire shame as a tool for discipline. Respect and relationship are the soil where growth happens. Children don't need to be shamed into goodness. They need to be loved into remembrance of who they already are.

As outlined in NAEYC's Developmentally Appropriate Practice, guidance should preserve children's dignity and view behavior through a developmental lens. Shame-based discipline, by contrast, undermines this dignity and leads to long-term harm.

Boundaries as Invitations

Boundaries, when offered with presence and clarity, are not restrictions. They are invitations to feel safe, to learn, to connect, and to grow within a world that makes sense.

As NAEYC (2020) reminds us, children thrive in environments where guidance is developmentally appropriate and delivered through nurturing, responsive relationships. Children don't need endless freedom to feel loved; they need consistent, compassionate boundaries to feel secure. When we set boundaries, we're not saying: "I don't love you." We are saying: "I love you enough to guide you."

Too often, adults confuse boundaries with control. But control seeks to dominate, usually rooted in fear, frustration, or a need to assert power. Boundaries seek to guide, offering the child a clear path forward while preserving dignity (Delahooke, 2019).

Boundaries also build trust. Children learn that adults will follow through—not in anger, but with steady guidance and support. Even when emotions run high, the relationship remains a safe space. Instead of simply saying "no," we can reframe the moment by:

- Naming what we see

- Stating what we want the child to do

- Explaining why it matters

For example: "I see you're climbing on the tables. I want to keep you safe, so please put your feet on the ground. I don't want you to fall and get hurt. We use tables for eating, playing games, and doing art."

This approach teaches respect and responsibility while reinforcing the purpose of the space and the adult's role as a guide, not just an enforcer. It invites cooperation rather than compliance.

And for many of us, this is healing work: to offer the kind of boundaries we never received. Boundaries that didn't come with cold silence or disconnection. Boundaries rooted not in fear, but in love.

Personal Reflection

Although I love my family deeply, I must name what has remained unspoken: I have never truly felt safe enough to tell my story.

Throughout my life, those around me only heard fragments—stories told through the voices of others. Insights shared not out of genuine curiosity, but through the lens of their own roles, whether raising me or growing up beside me. Rarely did anyone ask who I was beyond the surface, or what was stirring in my heart. My inner world remained unseen, not because I hid it, but because it was never truly invited to be seen.

Now, at this moment in my life, I am ready. I am prepared to share my story with those who are willing to listen—not the version others remember or retell, but mine.

Though I was raised to feel pride in my heritage, I often felt at odds with expectations, especially those that prioritized obedience over understanding. I was the child who asked "why" when silence was expected. The child who challenged the rules meant to be followed without question. I wouldn't quietly comply, and that, in many eyes, made me the "troublemaker."

To this day, family members still call me that label, often with a laugh, but it still cuts: "You never did what you were told." Behind the smile, I still hear the echo: You were too much.

What stayed with me wasn't rebellion. It was a shame—the quiet message that my curiosity and courage to speak up made me unworthy of understanding. That message etched itself into my sense of self for years.

This is why the work of setting boundaries without shame isn't just something I teach—it's something I live. It's deeply personal. Because I know what it feels like to be misunderstood, mislabeled, and minimized. And I know how transformative it is to be met with curiosity instead of control.

As educators, as parents, as humans, we are not just guiding behavior. We are shaping self-worth. Every word we speak to a child tells them something vital: "You are safe here," or "You are too much." Which will they remember? Let us choose our words and our presence with care. Because one moment of understanding can rewrite a lifetime of shame.

What Healthy Boundaries Actually Are

Healthy boundaries are not about control. They are about protecting space, safety, and connection. A developmentally appropriate boundary honors a child's need for expression and the community's need for safety (NAEYC, 2022).

Children can feel anger, sadness, and frustration. But not every action is acceptable. Hitting or destroying is not okay, not because the child is bad, but because the relationship matters. When we set a boundary, we are saying:

- "I care about you and our relationship enough to hold this line."

- "I will protect what matters, with love."

These boundaries are not punitive. They are protective. And they are most effective when delivered by a regulated adult who leads with empathy.

This aligns with Positive Discipline principles, which emphasize connection before correction and understanding the root cause of behavior (Nelsen, 2006). As DAP-aligned practice notes: "Limits should be developmentally realistic, clearly communicated, and modeled with consistency and kindness" (Copple & Bredekamp, 2009).

Professional Reflection

At the time of this story, I was overseeing eleven programs across the district. One site had recently undergone a difficult leadership transition. I had released the previous director due to an unfortunate incident, and during the interim period, I stepped in to support the team while we searched for a new director. Trust and stability were fragile, and I knew that how I responded in everyday moments would either restore or erode the culture we hoped to build.

During a visit to the school, a substitute teacher became visibly frustrated with a fourth-grade student named Ryan. From her perspective, Ryan was misusing materials, repeatedly sticking and peeling tape from the table surface. She saw the behavior as wasteful and disrespectful and was preparing to reprimand him.

Rather than correct him immediately, I paused and sat beside Ryan. "What are you working on?" I asked gently. Without hesitation, he looked up and said, "I'm trying to lift fingerprints."

In that instant, everything shifted. What had appeared to be defiance was actually curiosity—a spontaneous forensic science experiment in progress. I smiled and affirmed Ryan's creativity, sharing that what he was doing was part of real-world forensic science. I promised to bring in additional supplies the next day so we could explore the concept together.

Before moving on, though, I also held a boundary. "When tape is left stuck to the tables, it creates extra work for the teachers who clean the space," I explained calmly. "Could you be mindful and remove the tape when you're done next time?" Ryan nodded and smiled. He wasn't shamed or labeled; he was respected. And he responded with cooperation and pride.

The next day, as promised, I returned with charcoal powder and more tape. The entire class created fingerprint portfolios, discussed how everyone's prints are unique, and explored real-world connections to crime-solving and identity. What could have ended in disconnection and shame became a memory of excitement, curiosity, and respect.

The boundary was clear: use materials responsibly and clean up after yourself. But the delivery was compassionate. This is the heart of boundaries without shame—setting expectations without diminishing the child. It's not about letting things slide; it's about leading with dignity. Even now, I often find myself wondering if Ryan's spark for discovery led him to become a police officer or perhaps a forensic scientist.

When we hold boundaries with empathy, we teach children that accountability and creativity can coexist. By pausing to ask, "What were you trying to do?" or "Can we find a way that works better for everyone?" we build bridges rather than barriers. Boundaries without shame say: You are welcome here. Your voice matters. And we're learning how to live in this space together.

This lesson came to life again when a teacher shared the following story with me after one of my trainings.

Understanding the Why

A week or so after one of my trainings on not assuming malice in a child's behavior, a young pre-K teacher approached me with excitement. She explained that two boys had been climbing on a table—something she dealt with almost daily.

This time, instead of jumping straight to correction, she remembered the training and calmly asked herself, Why might they be doing this? She explained to the boys, "We have this rule to keep you safe and to keep the tables clean for lunchtime and playtime."

What happened next surprised her. Instead of the usual resistance or repeat behavior, the boys looked at her, nodded, and said, "Oh, okay." Then they climbed down and moved on to explore somewhere else. She told me, "That moment changed how I see everything. They weren't trying to be defiant, they just didn't understand why the rule existed."

This is why it is so important to pause, ask questions, and partner with children to help them understand the why behind the boundary. When children know the reason, they are far more likely to cooperate and to feel respected in the process.

Closing Thoughts

Children do not become more respectful by feeling less worthy. They do not become more accountable by feeling more afraid. Shame might create compliance in the moment, but it leaves behind wounds that echo for a lifetime.

When we choose to hold boundaries with kindness, we teach children how to remain whole in a world that often tries to fracture them. We teach them that love and limits can coexist.

And we begin—one interaction at a time—to rewrite the legacy. This is how we raise the next generation with dignity, strength, and a deep sense of belonging.

Chapter Eight
Honoring the Inner World of the Child

"Within every child is an entire universe, unseen and still forming. When we choose to honor their inner world, we do not shape them, we help them become who they uniquely already are." ~Debbie Hogue

In Chapter Seven, we explored boundaries without shame—how love and limits can coexist without fracturing a child's sense of self. Now, we go even deeper. Beneath every behavior is a world we can't always see. To truly guide and connect with children, we must learn to honor the vast inner worlds they carry.

Every Child Carries a World

Every child carries a world within them. Not just thoughts, not just feelings, but a rich, intricate tapestry of wonder, fear, hope, curiosity, and longing. Beneath every behavior lies a message. Beneath every outburst, a story. Beneath every silence, a language waiting to be heard (Greene, 2016; Perry & Szalavitz, 2006).

In our rush to correct or teach, we often overlook the quiet invitations children are offering: See me. Feel with me. Help me understand this storm inside. We confuse behavior with identity, mistake dysregulation for defiance, and forget that behind every reaction is a nervous system simply trying to cope, connect, or feel safe (Delahooke, 2019).

Children thrive in environments that reflect back what they most need inside: peace, rhythm, belonging, and safety. Their nervous systems are constantly scanning: "Am I safe here?" That answer is shaped not only by what we say but also by what the space itself communicates.

Our homes and classrooms either co-regulate or dysregulate. They can soothe or overstimulate, invite connection or trigger anxiety. As NAEYC (2020) emphasizes, emotionally responsive and predictable environments form the foundation for strong relationships, self-regulation, and lifelong learning.

And just as every child carries an inner world, so do we. To guide children well, we must first understand the landscapes we carry within ourselves—the unspoken stories, patterns, and wounds that shape the way we respond. This is where the work of tending to our own inner child begins.

A Child's Inner World

Children in my generation—Boomers and Gen-Xers—had a different kind of childhood. We were raised on: "Come home when the streetlights come on." We spent our days riding bikes, building forts out of anything we could find, and turning sticks and rocks into magical worlds. We didn't have structured playdates or curated toys. We had imagination, and we knew how to use it.

There were downsides to that era, including a lack of emotional awareness and support. But the freedom to create and explore? That was plentiful.

Years later, as a young mother, I found myself raising two daughters: one in second grade and the other in pre-K. I was learning about positive discipline, but I still found myself defaulting to the old ways I had inherited. Their shared bedroom was in constant chaos. Toys everywhere. Drawers emptied. Every warning to clean up was ignored. One day, I snapped.

I grabbed bins and packed away nearly every toy. "This is your consequence," I said. My youngest daughter still talks about that moment, how awful it felt to lose her toys. And if I'm being honest, I could've handled it differently. But what happened next surprised me.

Without their toys, the girls wandered outside. They collected leaves, rocks, and sticks. They built structures. Created characters. Invented games using nothing but their environment and imagination.

The front of our apartment became their kingdom. And as I watched them, I smiled. I saw in them a reflection of the child I once was. Surrounded not by plastic, but by possibility.

Eventually, I unpacked their toys. But the experience left an imprint—not just on them, but on me. It reminded me that children's inner worlds are always alive, always waiting, and often don't require more things to thrive. Sometimes, they just need space. To wonder. To create. To remember who they are without all the noise.

Holding Space Instead of Fixing

One of the greatest gifts we can give a child is the gift of presence without pressure. The kind that says: "I'm with you. I don't need to fix this. I just need to be here while you feel it."

As adults, it's hard not to rush in. We see a child upset, angry, or overwhelmed, and we instinctively want to soothe, solve, or stop the feeling. Not because we don't care, but because we care so much that it's uncomfortable to witness pain we can't immediately fix (Siegel & Bryson, 2011).

But children don't always need us to make it better. They need our help to hold it. Holding space means creating emotional safety without trying to rescue or redirect too quickly. It means resisting the urge to distract or "cheer up" and instead anchoring in empathy.

As Perry and Winfrey (2021) emphasize, the ability to co-regulate through attuned presence is more healing than any quick fix. Children build emotional resilience not by being pulled out of hard feelings, but by moving through them with someone they trust nearby.

Personal Reflection

After my daughter's husband left the military, they stayed with me for a while. One afternoon, I heard a commotion outside. My daughter was trying to get her son into the house.

On their way home, they had passed a neighbor's garage sale. My grandson had spotted something he wanted. Though my daughter bought him a small item, it wasn't enough. He wanted more.

When she told him no, disappointment turned into full-blown frustration. He was having a tantrum by the time they reached the door. My daughter handed my grandson to me and said, "Mom, can you deal with this?"

I calmly took him upstairs and asked him, "Do you want to read a book?" He wasn't having it and stood at the foot of the bed, yelling and stomping. I didn't respond with demands. I simply said, "It's okay. Just let me know when you're ready."

Then I opened the book, Green Eggs and Ham, and began reading aloud. Every now and then, I paused and asked, "Are you ready?" Each time, he growled, "No!" I didn't push. I just kept reading. After about five minutes, my grandson crawled onto the bed, snuggled in close, and whispered: "Let's start over." So we did.

That moment reminded me: Children don't always need fixing. They need someone steady enough to hold the space until they can return to connection. Sometimes, the most loving thing we can say is: "You don't have to go through this alone."

Emotional Literacy as a Birthright

If behavior is the language of the inner world, then emotional literacy is the key to translation. Children feel deeply from birth, but they aren't born with the words to describe what's happening inside.

Frustration becomes hitting. Loneliness becomes withdrawal. Overwhelm becomes shutdown. Without emotional vocabulary, they express what they cannot yet name (Denham, 2007). Emotional literacy is not a bonus. It's a birthright.

Teaching children to understand their emotions doesn't just help them regulate—it helps them feel seen. When we give children language for their feelings, we provide them with agency over their inner experience (CASEL, 2023). Emotional literacy includes:

- Recognizing what emotions feel like in the body

- Naming emotions with accuracy (not just "mad," but "frustrated," "disappointed," or "embarrassed")

- Understanding that emotions are not destructive—they are information

- Learning how to express feelings safely and respectfully

This work happens in ordinary moments:

- Through picture books and storytelling

- Using feeling charts or mirrors

- During co-regulation: "You look like you're feeling disappointed. I'm here with you."

- By modeling emotional honesty ourselves: "I feel overwhelmed right now, so I'm going to take a breath."

When we treat emotions with reverence instead of resistance, children learn that their inner world is not something to fear—it's something to explore. From that awareness, emotional intelligence blooms.

Professional Reflection

There was a day when several teachers were out, so I stepped in to help supervise lunch recess. As I scanned the playground, my eyes landed on a group of boys huddled together. Something about the energy felt... intense. Though nothing had gone wrong yet, I could feel something brewing, so I walked over to check in.

What I discovered was astonishing. These boys weren't misbehaving; they were governing. Over several months, they had quietly created their own country. They had a president, officers, and a council. They had drawn up rules, named their country, and even written a constitution. Their game had structure, diplomacy, and consequences. And they had kept it hidden from teachers out of fear it would be shut down.

In many schools, it would have been. But what I saw wasn't a threat; it was a glimpse into the extraordinary richness of their inner world. They weren't just playing—they were applying. They were taking the lessons they had learned in their history and government classes and bringing them to life in a way that felt alive and real.

That said... things had taken a dramatic turn. There was now talk of assassination and government overthrow, and for safety and ethics, we had to step in. But instead of shutting it down with punishment, I chose something else.

First, I praised them. I told them how impressed I was with their vision, their initiative, and their ability to create an entire functioning society. Then I said, "If you want this city to continue, you'll need to write a proposal. Show us your structure, your laws, and your purpose. Let's bring your teachers into this—not to end it, but to support it."

The spark returned to their eyes. This is what happens when we pause to listen and look beneath behavior. These boys weren't misbehaving; they were building worlds. They weren't power-hungry; they were exploring power dynamics the only way children can—through roleplay, imagination, and experimentation.

Children's inner worlds are vast and complex. When we meet them with curiosity instead of correction, we don't just keep them safe—we help them grow.

The Nervous System Speaks First

Before a child can explain what's wrong, before they can name their feelings, their nervous system has already sounded the alarm (Porges, 2011).

A fight might look like yelling or hitting. Flight might look like running or avoiding eye contact. Freeze might look like shutting down. Fawn might appear to be over-compliant or people-pleasing.

These are survival strategies. They are the body's way of trying to feel safe. Our role is to become the regulated anchor in a child's storm. Children borrow our calm. They learn safety not just from what we say, but from how we are—our tone, our breath, our presence.

Environments That Reflect Safety

Children feel safest in spaces that mirror their inner needs—calm, connection, predictability, and a sense of belonging. Their nervous systems are always attuned, asking: "Is this a safe place for me?" The answer lies not only in our words, but in the energy of the space itself—the tone, the rhythm, the atmosphere we create.

Our homes and classrooms either co-regulate or dysregulate. They can soothe or overstimulate, invite connection or trigger anxiety. As NAEYC (2020) emphasizes, emotionally responsive and predictable environments form the foundation for healthy development.

Safety is not just a sign on the wall. It's a felt sense that lives in the child's entire being. When the environment reflects that safety back to them, children begin to trust—not just the adult, but themselves.

Closing Thoughts

To truly honor a child's inner world is to recognize that they are not just minds to teach or bodies to care for. They are whole beings carrying more than we often imagine. We live in a culture that tends to define children by what they do, how they behave, and how quickly they meet milestones.

But what if we looked deeper? What if we saw beyond the tantrums, beyond the delays, beyond the diagnoses—and simply saw the child? When we treat children as individuals, we create space for them to flourish, not just conform. We help them become themselves, not just behave a certain way.

This is our deepest calling: Not just to teach children, but to remember them. To meet them not as problems to be solved, but as people to be cherished. And in doing so, we begin to remember ourselves.

Roots Series

Come grow with us

Chapter Nine

Beyond Grades and Standards

"True intelligence is not memorized, it's embodied. It's not the ability to recite, but the courage to wonder, to question, and to think beyond what is expected."
~Debbie Hogue

In Chapter Eight, we explored how children's inner worlds shape their behaviors, needs, and connections. We reminded ourselves to look beyond what we can see and honor the complexity of every child's emotions and nervous system. But our work doesn't end there.

Children eventually step into educational systems that often value performance over process and measurement over meaning. And when the brilliance we've nurtured meets rigid standards and narrow definitions of success, their inner worlds can be overshadowed by pressure and comparison.

This next chapter asks us to question those systems. It invites us to redefine intelligence, success, and learning itself so that children can thrive, not just survive, in the environments designed to "educate" them.

Redefining Success

From the moment a child enters school, an unspoken message begins to echo: Meet the standard. Earn the grade. Stay on pace.

Though often well-intentioned, this system reduces success to what can be measured rather than what can be lived. Intelligence becomes a number, growth becomes a benchmark, and curiosity—too often—becomes a disruption.

But children are not spreadsheets. Learning is not linear; it is dynamic and human. It unfolds in spirals, sparks, and detours. The children we serve carry within them not just potential, but brilliance—waiting to be seen in its own time and way.

Children learn best not when they are performing, but when they are engaged—mind, heart, and body. Real learning is not passive; it is alive. It is the messy process of wondering, trying, failing, and asking again. When we reduce it to correct answers and test scores, we rob children of the very thing that makes learning meaningful: connection.

Intelligence Wears Many Faces

Howard Gardner's theory of multiple intelligences (1983) reminds us that there are many ways to be "smart": linguistic, logical-mathematical, spatial, kinesthetic, musical, interpersonal, intrapersonal, and naturalistic. Yet traditional academic systems still overwhelmingly reward only a narrow few.

We see intelligence every day in the child who asks a question no one else thought to ask, in the student who struggles with math facts but can reassemble a broken toy with ease, in the daydreamer who sees connections others miss, and in the artist who expresses emotions on paper before they can find the words aloud.

Even in early childhood settings, where play and developmentally appropriate practice are emphasized, the pressure to "prepare" children for kindergarten has led to more formalized testing, early literacy benchmarks, and less unstructured exploration (Miller & Almon, 2009). This shift, while driven by policy and good intentions, can confuse compliance with competence. But compliance is not learning, and silence is not understanding.

Play Is Not a Break from Learning

The American Academy of Pediatrics (2018) affirms that play is not a break from learning; it is the highest form of learning for young children. Through play, children experiment with cause and effect, build executive function skills, negotiate socially, and develop creative problem-solving abilities. These are the accurate predictors of long-term success, not whether a child can sit still for extended periods or fill in the correct test bubble.

Moreover, standardized systems often fail to account for trauma, neurodivergence, cultural differences, and the emotional lives of children, all of which profoundly shape how they learn and express understanding (Delpit, 2012; Tager, 2019).

When we reframe success, we begin asking new questions:

- What brings this child to life?

- Where does their curiosity and joy live?

- How can we preserve their spirit while supporting their growth?

Reframing intelligence also means recognizing that memory and mastery are not the same. A child who can regurgitate information may still struggle with application, problem-solving, or interpersonal skills. Conversely, a child who cannot yet read fluently may be emotionally brilliant, spatially gifted, or deeply intuitive.

As educators, caregivers, and parents, our role is not to mold children into standard shapes. It is to notice their natural gifts and nourish them. The goal is to teach children that their identity is more critical than their accomplishments. It is to create environments where curiosity is not punished with red marks but welcomed with open minds. Where questions matter more than answers. Where wonder is a sign of brilliance, not distraction.

Personal Reflection

Years ago, after being laid off from an administrative (secretary) position, I was trying to figure out how to keep my oldest daughter in private kindergarten while staying home with my three-year-old.

During that time, the preschool director asked if I wanted to be a preschool teacher. Tuition would be free for my daughters, so I agreed.

After four days in the classroom, I honestly thought I had lost my mind. It was exhausting, chaotic, and unlike anything I had ever done before. But I stuck with it. And slowly, something shifted.

What started as a practical solution for my family soon became my calling. My journey into Early Childhood Education didn't begin because I intentionally set out to work in the field; it was born out of necessity. But as I watched the children in my care, I realized something important: if a mother had to work, she deserved to feel that her child was in a loving, safe, and supportive environment. That belief gave my work meaning and fueled my commitment to the children and families I served.

Not long after, my next chapter began. I moved to California, and that's when I started taking Early Childhood Education classes. My new partner at the time wasn't exactly supportive—he had a very high IQ and often made me feel small or ignorant by comparison—but I kept going. The more I learned, the more I grew, not just in knowledge, but in confidence.

For the first time in my life, I was earning straight A's. My professors believed in me, and each encouraging comment chipped away at the lie I had carried for years: that I wasn't "smart enough."

Although I still struggle with self-doubt at times, I've learned this: intelligence isn't about the labels others give you—it's about daring to rise anyway. And though Early Childhood Education is a predominantly female field, I soon realized it was exactly where I was meant to be. My experiences as a mother gave me a deep understanding of what families need most: to know their children are loved, supported, and truly seen.

The words and messages we give children matter. They linger for years, often for a lifetime. It's time to set every child up for success, not just by encouraging learning, but by helping them discover how they learn best. My youngest daughter did her best work while listening to music or watching TV. My oldest needed quiet and order. Neither was wrong; they were simply different.

As educators, caregivers, and parents, that's our charge: to see those differences, nurture passions, and remind children every day that who they are matters even more than what they can produce. This work became more than a career—it became my calling.

Redefining the Role of the Educator

If we are to move beyond grades and standards, we must reimagine what it means to teach.

Educators are not just deliverers of information. We are guides, mirrors, and nurturers of each child's innate way of learning. We protect curiosity. We create spaces where children are not compared to one another but connected to themselves.

Instead of asking, "Is this child meeting the standard?" we must ask, "How is this child growing right now?" Instead of "Are they on pace with peers?" we must ask, "What strengths are emerging at their own pace?"

This approach aligns with developmentally appropriate practices outlined by NAEYC (2020), which affirm that learning must be rooted in each child's needs, interests, and cultural background.

Some children need to move to think. Others need silence to process. Some need to talk things out; others prefer quiet reflection. Recognizing these differences isn't just a teaching strategy—it's a human responsibility.

Professional Reflection

My education journey was never part of a grand plan—it was something that found me. As I mentioned earlier, after being laid off from an administrative position in Dallas, I was trying to figure out how to keep my oldest child enrolled in kindergarten while caring for my three-year-old. One day, while visiting the school, the director asked me a question that would change the course of my life: "Would you be interested in working with preschoolers?"

I had no idea at the time that this unexpected invitation would set the stage for my life's greatest passion. If I couldn't stay home with my own children, I wanted to be somewhere that truly mattered. Deep in my soul, I believed that if mothers had to work, they deserved to know their children were in loving, safe, and supportive environments. That conviction became the foundation for everything I would do in this field.

Over my 30-year journey, I've worked within a wide range of learning environments: public schools, HighScope, Head Start programs (including Pre-K at Vogel Alcove), play-based programs like KinderCare and Goddard, Reggio Emilia-inspired and emergent programs like Stanford, and academically rigorous institutions like Primrose and Stratford. These experiences taught me something invaluable: success in early childhood education has never been determined by the model or the label. It has always come down to relationships.

It comes down to how teachers connect with children, how administrators support teachers, and how schools partner with families. This is what truly creates the conditions for growth.

Parents often worry that their child is not learning "fast enough" in reading, math, or science. These fears are understandable and usually rooted in the pressures they experienced growing up—pressures from a culture that equates success with performance and comparison. But development is not linear; it does not move in perfect, predictable steps. It follows the child.

When educators help families understand typical developmental progressions, we shift the lens from worry to understanding. We begin to see each child as they are, not as we fear they might fall short. That shift, from fear to trust, is one of the most powerful gifts we can offer families.

Research Integration

Research continues to affirm what educators witness daily: when we prioritize holistic development over performance-based outcomes, children thrive.

- Hart & Risley (1995) found that early language exposure and emotionally responsive environments—not formal instruction—were the strongest predictors of academic success.

- OECD (2019) emphasizes that non-cognitive skills such as self-regulation, empathy, and adaptability are equally critical to lifelong achievement.

- Dr. Yong Zhao (2016) advocates for personalized learning that nurtures creativity and global competence rather than ranking students by standardized metrics.

When children feel safe, seen, and valued for who they are—not just for how they perform—they become more resilient, curious, and capable learners.

Closing Thoughts

Let us create classrooms, homes, and communities where children are not defined by outdated systems, but set free by understanding. Let us teach as though every child is a story unfolding. Let us believe that every child is already enough. Because success is not a finish line.

It is a felt sense of purpose, belonging, and becoming. And in the end, children are not just watching—they are becoming.

Chapter Ten
Teaching with Purpose and Presence

*"The heart of teaching is not found in standards or
assessments, but in presence. Every moment with a child
is an invitation to either deepen or diminish their sense of worth."*
~Debbie Hogue

In Chapter Nine, we challenged the rigid systems that reduce children's brilliance to grades, benchmarks, and comparisons. We redefined success as something far more profound than performance—a sense of purpose, belonging, and becoming.

But knowing what children need is only the first step. How we show up for them, every single day, is what turns these ideals into lived experiences.

Because children don't just need new systems. They need adults who model what it means to live with presence, purpose, and compassion. This next chapter is about that presence—and the profound impact it can have.

Teaching with Purpose and Presence

Teaching is often described as a profession, a vocation, or even a calling. But for those who have spent their lives walking beside children, we know it is something even deeper.

Teaching with purpose and presence has the power to heal generational wounds, restore fractured identities, and help children rise fully into themselves. Children do not just need information. They need relationships. They need adults who:

- Model kindness and authenticity.

- Show what it looks like to make mistakes and repair them.

- Listen deeply, beyond the behavior or checklist.

- See the heart of the child before them.

Every interaction shapes the emotional architecture of a life. A raised eyebrow can shame. A smile can soothe. A harsh tone can fracture trust. A moment of empathy can open a door that has long been closed.

When children are met with authenticity, flexibility, and care, they internalize the belief that they are worthy, that they matter, and that their voice belongs.

The Impact of Teacher Presence

A consistent, emotionally attuned teacher can transform a child's experience in school. Research from the Center on the Developing

Child at Harvard (2016) shows that supportive adult relationships are one of the most important protective factors in a child's life. They buffer stress, build resilience, and help children develop executive functioning skills. Teacher presence is not about perfection. It is about being grounded and authentic. When teachers:

- Acknowledge their mistakes,

- Share emotions appropriately, and

- Set clear yet flexible boundaries,

They create psychologically safe environments where children feel free to take risks, ask questions, and be themselves (Immordino-Yang & Damasio, 2007).

Flexibility matters too. Classrooms ruled by rigid expectations may look orderly, but they often suppress creativity and independence. In contrast, classrooms with structure and responsiveness foster stronger engagement, deeper problem-solving, and healthier relationships (Hamre & Pianta, 2005).

Modeling Regulation and Repair

One of the most powerful teaching strategies isn't a lesson plan or a behavior chart—it's the ability to regulate yourself and model repair. Children watch adults closely. They learn not only what we say, but how we act when things don't go as planned.

This is the concept of rupture and repair, well documented in developmental psychology. Misattunement is inevitable, but repairing those moments builds trust and shows children that relationships can hold imperfection (Tronick, 2007). In practice, this might look like:

- Saying, "I raised my voice earlier. That wasn't the best way to handle it. I'm sorry, and I want to try again."

- Sitting beside a child after a difficult moment, not to reprimand but to reconnect.

- Narrating calm strategies out loud: "I'm going to take a few deep breaths so I can be ready to help again."

These moments model emotional intelligence in real time and build a culture of psychological safety.

Personal Reflection

In seventh grade, I loved science. One of my favorite projects was determining our blood types—mine was O negative. I remember being so curious and engaged during that lesson. Science was hands-on and exciting, and as someone who had just made the cheerleading team that year, it was also a fun way to connect with peers.

But I'll admit, at that stage, having made the cheerleading squad that year, I was far more focused on popularity than performance. What I didn't realize at the time was that I was probably a bit of a challenge in the classroom. I was social, chatty, and easily distracted by friends.

After a parent-teacher conference, my mom told my teacher he could send me to the office for corporal punishment if needed (something that was still allowed then). She even said that if I received it at school, I would get another session at home.

His response surprised her: "I don't want to do that. She only misbehaves when I cross her." Instead of punishment, he chose understanding. My mom's reply was blunt: "Then you deserve what you get if you're not willing to discipline her."

Looking back, I don't remember being defiant, though my priorities were clearly elsewhere that year. What stood out wasn't what I did wrong—it was what my teacher did right. He saw me. He inspired me.

I don't remember the lessons he taught from the curriculum, but I remember him—his presence, his care, and his refusal to shame me. That experience left a lasting imprint. It shaped the kind of teacher and leader I aspire to be: one who sees beyond behavior and chooses connection over control.

The Educator as a Regulator

Teachers set the emotional tone of the classroom. This isn't metaphorical—it's physiological. Neuroscience shows that children's nervous systems are constantly scanning their environment for cues of safety or threat (Porges, 2011).

A calm, attuned adult signals safety. An emotionally reactive or unavailable adult can trigger a child's survival brain, shutting down higher-order thinking (Siegel, 2012).

This is the concept of co-regulation: when an emotionally regulated adult helps stabilize a child's stress response. When teachers understand their role as nervous system anchors, they begin to prioritize their own regulation as a professional responsibility. Practices like deep breathing, pausing before responding, or even small moments of reflection directly benefit both the teacher and the children.

Professional Reflection

Throughout my 30-year career working with children—from infants to fifth grade—I've had countless opportunities to encourage growth, guide behavior, and support emotional development. These lessons have come not only from my time in schools but from experiences at home, too.

One moment that has always stayed with me is the story of a kindergarten student who had been labeled "a bad kid" by some of the adults around him. We'll call him Jacob.

Jacob was five years old, often angry, and frequently overwhelmed. One day, after a particularly difficult outburst, his teacher brought him to the office. I invited him to step into the nurse's office with me. As we walked in, one of the administrators quietly pulled me aside and said, "Be careful. He can get aggressive." I nodded and replied gently, "It's okay. I've got this."

Inside the office, Jacob sat on the floor, his small body consumed by emotion. He yelled and kicked, unable to regulate himself. I didn't respond with demands or consequences. I simply sat quietly and said, "It's okay. I'm here when you're ready."

Then I picked up a shark book nearby and began to read aloud—not to him, but just aloud. A few moments later, I noticed the energy in the room shift. Jacob quieted. Slowly, he stood and came to sit beside me. "That's the shark I'm going to be in our class performance," he said, pointing at a page.

I smiled. "Which one?" I asked. He leaned closer and proudly showed me. We stayed there a few more minutes, sharing the book, talking about sea creatures, and simply being together. When he was ready, we walked back to class side by side. He returned to the group without any resistance.

That moment reminded me of something I had first learned with my grandson: children don't always need correction. Sometimes they just need to feel a connection. When we show up with presence instead of punishment, we don't just de-escalate a situation—we help a child come back to themselves.

Yes, one dysregulated child can disrupt an entire classroom. But one meaningful, regulated adult can shift the energy of the whole room. Teachers who respond with empathy show not only the child but the entire class what safety looks like in practice. That's how we change the story for everyone.

Science, Standards, and the Power of Presence

Modern brain science affirms what great educators have always known: learning is relational. Children learn best when they feel safe, valued, and connected (National Scientific Council on the Developing Child, 2020).

NAEYC (2020) emphasizes that teachers foster learning and development through thoughtful, intentional interactions that are:

- Emotionally supportive

- Culturally responsive

- Cognitively stimulating

Perfection isn't required. Presence is.

Closing Thoughts

Teaching with purpose and presence is about more than delivering lessons. It's about shaping lives. When we:

- Show up authentically, and we give children permission to be themselves.

- Remain flexible, we teach them how to bend instead of break.

- Care deeply and consistently, we offer them something they will carry for life—the felt experience of being seen, supported, and safe.

This is how we shift from control to connection, from reaction to reflection, from performance to purpose. Because every child we teach is becoming. And every moment of presence leaves a legacy.

Chapter Eleven

Co-Regulation in the Classroom

"Children don't become calm because we tell them to. They become calm because we show them how." ~Debbie Hogue

In Chapter Ten, we explored how the presence of a teacher can shape a child's sense of safety, trust, and belonging. Presence is not simply about being in the room; it is about how we show up.

Co-regulation takes this presence a step further. It is the living, daily practice of helping children calm their nervous systems so they can feel secure enough to learn, grow, and connect.

The Practice of Nervous System Safety

Co-regulation is not a program or a curriculum. It isn't a poster on the wall or a 10:15 lesson followed by a worksheet. Co-regulation is a living practice. It happens in the micro-moments:

- When a teacher softens their voice.

- When a child is met with a reassuring glance.

- When the pace of the day slows to meet the group's needs.

In many schools, social-emotional learning (SEL) is treated as an isolated subject taught during circle time or through character-building curricula. While those efforts are important, they often fall short if the adults don't embody the skills throughout the day. Children don't learn emotional regulation because we tell them about it. They learn it because they experience it.

The Science of Co-Regulation

Co-regulation is the process by which an emotionally regulated adult helps a child return to a state of calm. It is foundational, not optional. Dr. Stephen Porges' Polyvagal Theory (2011) explains that children's nervous systems are constantly scanning their environment for cues of safety—a subconscious process called neuroception.

When a child senses danger (even emotional danger), the brain shifts into survival mode: fight, flight, freeze, or fawn. In this state, learning is nearly impossible because the brain is prioritizing protection over cognition.

This is where a calm, grounded adult makes all the difference. Through tone, body posture, facial expression, and proximity, the adult's nervous system communicates: "You are safe. You are not alone. We can figure this out together."

Co-regulation is not about perfection. It's about awareness. When teachers model emotional regulation, they invite children into a felt experience of safety. Over time, that felt experience builds the child's own capacity for self-regulation.

What Co-Regulation Looks Like

- Kneeling to eye level and speaking slowly when a child is distressed.

- Naming emotions with empathy: "That was really frustrating. I get it. Let's take a breath together."

- Creating calm-down corners or regulation spaces in the classroom can help students manage their emotions.

- Using rhythmic routines, songs, or breathing exercises to help the group reset.

These moments are not separate from learning. They are the foundation of knowledge.

Personal Story

My grandson was a fearless four-year-old. One day, he began leaping off the stairs at home, higher and higher each time. Naturally, I grew concerned and asked him to stop, worried he might get hurt.

My request triggered an immediate explosion of emotion. My grandson growled, yelled, and clenched his fists in anger. Instead of scolding him, I simply named what I saw: "I see that you are so mad!"

Then I had a light bulb moment, an idea. I turned on the song that I knew my grandson loved, Bad to the Bone. I started dancing with my best friend, we were growling and moving to the rhythm. My grandson froze for a moment, watching us. And then, just like that, he joined in. He growled, danced, and laughed until tears filled his eyes. His anger melted into joy—not because I controlled the moment, but because I connected with him in it.

That memory has stayed with me for years. It taught me a truth I've carried into my professional life: children don't need us to eliminate big emotions; they need us to move through those emotions together. Anger is a valid emotion. What children need most in those moments isn't correction—it's connection.

Sometimes, co-regulation looks like rhythm, laughter, and play.

Group Energy and Emotional Contagion

Emotions don't exist in isolation. Just as one child's distress can ripple outward, a teacher's calm can ripple too. Psychologists call this emotional contagion—the subconscious way we "catch" one another's emotions (Hatfield, Cacioppo, & Rapson, 1994).

A classroom is a living emotional ecosystem, and the adult at the center sets the tone. One dysregulated adult can escalate the group's stress. But one regulated adult can help steady everyone. Practical strategies for group regulation:

- Start and end the day with consistent rituals children can count on.

- Build in whole-group breathing or movement breaks to reset energy.

- Reduce sensory clutter—visual noise and loud environments spike stress.

- Create a "soft start" to the day by prioritizing connection before instruction.

Classrooms that practice group regulation are often quieter, not because children are silenced, but because they feel safe.

The Power of Predictability

Children thrive when they know what to expect. Predictable routines allow the nervous system to relax and stay open to learning.

- Greet each child warmly at the door.

- Use visual schedules and review them together each morning.

- Keep transitions rhythmic and familiar.

- Stay emotionally consistent, even when the child's behavior is unpredictable.

This type of structure doesn't restrict freedom; it creates safety.

Professional Reflection

When I worked as a Program Specialist for the school district, one of my responsibilities was to support various after-school programs by stepping in when a site director was out sick or on vacation. During one such assignment, I encountered a group of fourth-grade girls isolating themselves in the dramatic play area. They had built a barricade and were refusing to let other children, especially boys, enter their space.

At first, I tried a few conventional methods to redirect the behavior, but nothing worked. So I shifted my approach. I calmly stepped over the barricade and sat down in the middle of their circle. "What's going on?" I asked gently.

The girls opened up. They were tired of being in after-school care. They felt too old for the program and just wanted to be home. I validated their frustration and acknowledged their feelings. Then I reminded them that their parents were working hard to provide a home, food, and clothes, and that being in the program was part of keeping them safe while their parents worked. After a pause, I asked them a simple question: "What do you consider fun?"

Their faces lit up. They told stories about sleepovers and making pancakes for their families, laughing about the messes they made. That was my opening. I invited them to help design our weekly snack menus and assist in preparing the food.

The next day, we made pancakes together. Initially, the girls wanted to exclude the boys from the experience. I didn't force inclusion, but

I asked a reflective question: "How does it feel when someone doesn't include you?" We talked through the emotions. Without being told what to do, they chose to invite one of the boys. From that moment forward, inclusion happened naturally.

That experience wasn't just a lesson in emotional intelligence. It became an opportunity for the children to practice real-life math, sequencing, collaboration, and empathy. It reminded me that co-regulation isn't just about helping children calm down—it's about creating an environment where connection fosters cooperation, and where emotional safety becomes the foundation for growth and learning.

In early childhood education, we often speak of unconditional acceptance, of seeing the whole child, honoring their uniqueness, and creating spaces where they feel safe, valued, and loved. But that same principle must also extend to the teachers we bring into the classroom.

Several years ago, I interviewed a young man named Ben for a teaching position at a preschool I was supporting in Dallas, Texas. He was thoughtful, passionate, and deeply connected to his "why." He had the kind of natural presence that can't be taught, the ability to meet children where they are and gently guide them into who they are becoming. But not everyone saw it.

The school owner wasn't sure hiring a male teacher was "a good idea." It was a hesitation I had heard before, rooted in outdated fears, quiet bias, and unconscious gender roles still embedded in the early childhood field. This time, I pushed back. I advocated. I stood firmly in what I knew: that children deserve to see love, care, and leadership from adults of all genders and that the field of education needs the voices of those too often pushed to its edges. Eventually, I was given the green light to hire him. Years later, I received a message from this young man I will never forget, one that touched my heart in a way I cannot fully explain:

> "You were the first person to give me a shot in the education field when you worked at Primrose, especially when I was getting denied for simply being a man. I'll forever appreciate you for that."

His words reminded me that advocacy isn't always loud. Sometimes it's a quiet stand taken in a staff meeting or behind a closed office door. Sometimes it's a single hiring decision, made in alignment with a deeper knowing. Sometimes, it's the simple "yes" we offer to someone when the world keeps saying no.

As educational leaders, we are not just shaping classrooms; we are shaping the profession. The future of early childhood education depends on our willingness to question norms, release bias, and expand our definition of who gets to be a teacher.

The same acceptance we so freely offer children must be extended to the adults who teach them. Because when we believe in a teacher, we're not just changing their life, we're changing every life they will go on to touch.

The Science and Standards Behind SEL

Co-regulation is not an "extra." It is a biologically informed, developmentally appropriate necessity. Neuroscientists like Dr. Bruce Perry and Dr. Daniel Siegel remind us that relationships are the context in which the brain develops. Safety and connection are not rewards for good behavior; they are prerequisites for learning.

The National Association for the Education of Young Children reinforces this truth: "Strong relationships help children feel secure and supported, which is essential for learning and development."

Cognitive and social-emotional development are interdependent. A child in distress cannot learn. And a child who feels emotionally safe can take risks, collaborate, and engage deeply with academics.

Closing Thoughts

To truly teach SEL, we must live it. The work of co-regulation isn't just about calming the storm in the moment; it's about building a foundation of safety that carries children through their entire learning journey. Which brings us here: to the bigger vision of educating the whole child. Because when we see and support children fully—head, heart, and hands—we do more than teach; we help them flourish.

Chapter Twelve

The Whole Child, The Whole Future

"We are not just preparing children for tests. We are preparing them for life and the lives they will touch."
~Debbie Hogue

In Chapter Eleven, we explored how co-regulation is not just a classroom strategy, but a living practice—one that shapes the emotional climate where children learn. This final chapter takes that same principle even further. Because when we expand our lens beyond individual moments and see the child in their fullness—their body, mind, heart, and spirit—we begin to understand what it truly means to educate the whole child.

Educating the whole child means recognizing that children are not just brains to be filled or behaviors to be managed; they are entire individuals with unique needs, perspectives, and ways of being. They are emotional, physical, creative, spirited, and social beings.

When we honor the whole child, we see beyond test scores and checklists. We acknowledge their voices, their rhythms, their emotions, and their full humanity. We stop teaching to the standard, and we start teaching to the child.

In countries like Finland and Japan, education systems integrate movement, reflection, nature, and emotional regulation throughout the day. Movement breaks are not treated as a reward for compliance; they are embedded because research shows that physical activity improves focus, emotional regulation, and executive functioning. According to the CDC (2010), even brief movement breaks during class enhance cognitive performance and improve on-task behavior.

When children are given time to move, stretch, reset, and breathe, their bodies feel safe, and their brains remain alert. Yet in many U.S. classrooms, the pressure to meet benchmarks often leads to fewer breaks and extended seated work, despite mounting evidence that movement enhances learning rather than disrupts it.

We must shift the narrative: children are not learning machines. They are developing humans with dynamic nervous systems. And movement isn't a disruption to learning—it's a return to it.

This final chapter is both a reflection and a call to action: an invitation to rise into a new kind of leadership, one that integrates compassion, cognition, and structure. The future we want begins with how we choose to see and support the whole child today.

The Integration of Head, Heart, and Hands

Whole-child education designs learning environments that develop intellect (head), cultivate empathy and emotional intelligence (heart), and encourage meaningful action and creativity (hands). It's not about sacrificing academic rigor; it's about embedding it within a framework that honors each learner's humanity.

The OECD's Future of Education and Skills 2030 project emphasizes that children need more than literacy and numeracy to thrive in an unpredictable world. They need agency, adaptability, and a deep sense of belonging and purpose (OECD, 2018). These capacities are not cultivated through rigid instruction, but through trust, engagement, and integrated experiences. In early childhood and elementary settings, this might look like:

- A literacy lesson that invites children to share personal stories and build emotional vocabulary.

- A math activity infused with movement, collaboration, and real-world problem-solving.

- Science experiments are born from children's questions about the world around them.

- Classrooms where reflection, journaling, or "feelings check-ins" are part of the daily rhythm.

This integrated learning reflects what educational theorists like John Dewey and Maria Montessori championed: children learn best when they are actively engaged in meaningful, connected experiences. Modern neuroscience confirms this: when children feel safe and emotionally invested, their brains form deeper, more lasting connections to the material.

NAEYC emphasizes that developmentally appropriate practice involves the intentional integration of cognitive, social-emotional, and physical development. When teachers allow children to think, feel, and move as part of the learning process, they honor the whole child and maximize growth.

Personal Reflection

As both a mother and grandmother, I have seen firsthand how challenging it can be to support children's academic journeys, especially when they don't fit traditional molds.

My youngest daughter always had music or the TV on while she did homework. I constantly asked her to turn it off, believing that silence was the only way to focus. One day in eighth grade, frustrated, she looked at me and said, "Mom, the music helps me focus."

That moment stopped me. I stepped back and trusted my daughter's process. Sure enough, she completed her big Argentina project with focus and pride. The real lesson for me wasn't about the project at all; it was about letting go of my assumptions and listening to what she needed to succeed.

By high school, it was clear that traditional school wasn't the best fit. My daughter enrolled in a community college early-college program, finished her last three years of high school there, and thrived with the autonomy and flexibility. She even gave a speech at her high school graduation, a moment that reflected not just academic success, but the confidence and leadership she had grown into by following her own path.

My grandson has had a similar journey. Brilliant and creative, he struggled in rigid systems that misunderstood him. His parents homeschooled him at times during early years, giving him space to learn at his own pace. Today, he is thriving in online learning because the environment finally meets his needs.

These experiences taught me that the one-size-fits-all approach doesn't work. When we honor learning styles, pacing, and emotional needs, we are not lowering expectations. We are raising the standard for what it truly means to educate.

Movement, Memory, and Mind: What Research Says

Cognitive neuroscience is clear: movement is not just beneficial, it is essential. Physical activity increases blood flow to the brain, boosts neurotransmitters like dopamine and serotonin, and strengthens neural pathways connected to memory, attention, and emotional regulation (Ratey, 2008).

A 2013 study in Frontiers in Psychology found that regular movement breaks significantly improved working memory and executive function, especially in younger children.

Other countries have already integrated this into practice. In Finland, students enjoy 15-minute breaks for every 45 minutes of instruction, often outdoors. Teachers report fewer behavior challenges and higher engagement (Sahlberg, 2015).

In Japan, daily school life includes movement through group exercises, mindfulness practices, and frequent transitions, promoting cohesion and emotional stability.

Meanwhile, many U.S. classrooms still withhold recess as punishment, and children spend six or more hours a day sitting. But the evidence is overwhelming: the body and brain learn together. Movement reduces stress hormones, increases focus, and improves learning outcomes.

NAEYC reinforces this approach, noting that cognitive, physical, and emotional development are deeply interconnected. Teachers who weave movement, play, and social interaction into their daily rhythm don't just support development—they unlock it.

Professional Reflection

I have walked into hundreds of classrooms over my career. Some radiated freedom and joy. Others felt heavy with pressure. And many fell somewhere in between.

One memory stands out: a teacher was overwhelmed by constant behavior struggles. Her schedule was rigid, transitions rushed, and she felt like the children never listened. I asked a straightforward question: "Have you tried letting them move first?"

We carved out three 10-minute movement breaks each day—dancing, stretching, and quick games. The transformation was remarkable. The children became more regulated, transitions smoother, and the teacher began to smile again.

This reminded me, once more, that whole-child education isn't about doing more. It's about doing what matters most. When we shift from control to connection, children feel better. When they feel better, they learn better.

I saw this powerfully in the Reggio Emilia-inspired curriculum I helped implement at Stanford's early childhood programs. Reggio's image of the child as capable and its emphasis on rich environments resonated deeply with me.

Yet after my time at Stratford's San Jose campus—a balanced but academically rigorous program—I gained a more profound truth: it's not the philosophy that makes or breaks the classroom. It's the teacher. The curriculum is the framework, but the teacher is the heartbeat.

Parents, too, must feel empowered to pivot when a school or program doesn't meet their child's needs. True education is not about forcing children to stay on one track; it's about helping them find the path that allows them to thrive.

Science, Vision, and the Road Ahead

The science is precise: relationships, rhythm, movement, and emotional safety are not extras—they are essential. The Collaborative for Academic, Social, and Emotional Learning (CASEL, 2023) found that students in strong SEL programs saw an average 11-percentile-point gain on standardized achievement tests, as well as stronger classroom behavior and stress management.

Harvard's Center on the Developing Child (2020) describes "serve and return" interactions—back-and-forth exchanges between adults and children—as the building blocks of brain architecture. These relationships are the foundation of learning.

Movement also continues to stand out. Students who are more physically active have better GPAs, improved attendance, and stronger classroom behavior (Rasberry et al., 2011). We must remember: the whole child holds the entire future. When we teach in ways that embrace body, mind, and heart, we are not only increasing academic performance—we are cultivating purpose.

Closing Thoughts

The future of education does not live in higher test scores or tighter control. It lives in our ability to see children in their fullness. It lives in our courage to change course when the old systems no longer serve. It lives in our willingness to lead with heart, reflection, and deep trust in the child before us.

There is no one-size-fits-all model. But there is one unshakable truth: when children feel safe, seen, and supported, they learn. They rise. They remember.

Let us be the ones who remember, too. Let us build classrooms and communities that honor the whole child. Because in doing so, we shape not just better learners, but more compassionate humans.

And that—more than anything—is the future worth creating.

Afterword
This Legacy, Now Yours to Pass On

The Last Word

This moment invites us to remember:
Every child carries echoes of the adult they will become.
Every adult holds a memory of the child they once were.
Healing flows both ways when we truly see each other.

This is not just the end of a book;
it is a soft beginning of something greater.
A call to remember the child within, the adult beside us,
and the ancestors whose voices echo in our stories.

You hold the pen now. You are the bridge. You are the rewrite.
Let this be your new beginning.

References

References and Supporting Literature

Afifi, T. D., Joseph, A., & Aldeis, D. (2017). The impact of harsh parenting on child outcomes. Journal of Family Communication, 17(4), 323–340.

Baumrind, D. (1991). The influence of parenting style on adolescent competence and substance use. Journal of Early Adolescence, 11(1), 56–95.

Brackett, M. (2019). Permission to feel. Celadon Books.

Brown, B. (2010). The gifts of imperfection. Hazelden Publishing.

CASEL. (2023). Core SEL competencies. Collaborative for Academic, Social, and Emotional Learning. https://casel.org

Centers for Disease Control and Prevention. (2010). The association between school-based physical activity and academic performance. U.S. Department of Health and Human Services.

Delahooke, M. (2019). Beyond behaviors: Using brain science and compassion to understand and solve children's behavioral challenges. PESI Publishing.

Dweck, C. S. (2006). Mindset: The new psychology of success. Random House.

Greene, R. W. (2016). The explosive child. HarperCollins.

Hamre, B. K., & Pianta, R. C. (2001). Early teacher–child relationships and the trajectory of children's school outcomes. Child Development, 72(2), 625–638.

Hillman, C. H., Erickson, K. I., & Kramer, A. F. (2014). Be smart, exercise your heart: Exercise effects on brain and cognition. Nature Reviews Neuroscience, 9(1), 58–65.

Maté, G. (2019). The myth of normal: Trauma, illness, and healing in a toxic culture. Avery.

National Association for the Education of Young Children. (2020). Developmentally appropriate practice in early childhood programs serving children from birth through age 8 (4th ed.). https://naeyc.org/resources/position-statements/dap

OECD. (2018). The future of education and skills: Education 2030. Organisation for Economic Co-operation and Development. https://www.oecd.org/education/2030/

Perry, B. D., & Szalavitz, M. (2006). The boy who was raised as a dog: And other stories from a child psychiatrist's notebook. Basic Books.

Perry, B. D., & Winfrey, O. (2021). What happened to you? Conversations on trauma, resilience, and healing. Flatiron Books.

Porges, S. W. (2011). The polyvagal theory: Neurophysiological foundations of emotions, attachment, communication, and self-regulation. W. W. Norton & Company.

Rasberry, C. N., Lee, S. M., Robin, L., Laris, B. A., Russell, L. A., Coyle, K. K., & Nihiser, A. J. (2011). The association between school-based physical activity, including physical education, and academic performance: A systematic review of the literature. Journal of Pediatrics, 158(5), 721–728.

Ratey, J. J. (2008). Spark: The revolutionary new science of exercise and the brain. Little, Brown Spark.

Sahlberg, P. (2015). Finnish lessons 2.0: What can the world learn from educational change in Finland? Teachers College Press.

Seay, K. D., Freysteinson, W. M., & McFarlane, J. (2014). Positive parenting: A meta-analysis of parenting programs using social learning theory. Journal of Pediatric Health Care, 28(3), 226–233.

Shanker, S. (2016). Self-reg: How to help your child (and you) break the stress cycle and successfully engage with life. Penguin.

Siegel, D. J., & Bryson, T. P. (2011). The whole-brain child: 12 revolutionary strategies to nurture your child's developing mind. Delacorte Press.

Siegel, D. J., & Hartzell, M. (2003). Parenting from the inside out. TarcherPerigee.

About the Author

Voice of the Roots Rewritten Series
Where Healing Begins with Awareness

Debbie Hogue is a seasoned early childhood educator, mentor, and advocate with over 30 years of experience guiding programs that support the emotional, developmental, and academic needs of children from infancy through the school-age years. Her journey began in a small Texas preschool and has since expanded across public and private sectors, including leadership roles at Stanford University and Santa Clara Unified School District, where she built inclusive, nationally accredited programs rooted in compassion, equity, and connection.

From her early days as a teacher's aide to becoming a lead teacher, director, and area leader, Debbie has shaped the landscape of early education by mentoring hundreds of educators, securing accreditations, and supporting families across diverse communities, including those navigating poverty and homelessness. Her approach is grounded in research-based practices, including Positive Discipline, Developmentally Appropriate Practice (DAP), and trauma-informed care.

Debbie holds a formal education in both child development and business management and has contributed to national conversations through advisory work with Wellesley College and NAEYC-aligned training initiatives. She brings not only professional expertise but also a deep heart, believing that lasting change begins when adults pause, reflect, and choose a more conscious path.

Her first book, Roots Rewritten, is an offering to those ready to break generational cycles and create emotionally safe, respectful environments where children can truly thrive.

Debbie currently resides in Prescott Valley, Arizona. She is the proud mother of two daughters and grandmother to eight grandchildren. She continues to write, speak, and mentor the next generation of educators and caregivers with a steadfast commitment to rewriting the way we nurture childhood.

She is also the founder of Ink of Becoming Publications, an independent press dedicated to uplifting soul-centered stories, healing journeys, and transformative voices that honor both legacy and change.

www.ingramcontent.com/pod-product-compliance
Lightning Source LLC
Chambersburg PA
CBHW062124040426
42337CB00044B/3959